No, We're Not
a Funny
Bunch of People!

Johnny Lancaster

NO, WE'RE NOT A FUNNY BUNCH OF PEOPLE

ISBN 1 85863 090 8

First Published 1993 by
MINERVA PRESS
2, Old Brompton Road,
London SW7 3DQ.

Second Impression 1994

Printed in Great Britain by
Martins Printers Ltd., Berwick upon Tweed.

"With thanks."

As there have been many people who have helped me, in various ways, with the writing of this book, I am not going to single any individual out, but merely evince gratitude to all concerned. I trust that they will enjoy the end result and accept my sincere thanks for all they have done. It will be my future pleasure to raise my glass in their presence.

To the memory of my proposer and seconder, Wor. Bro. Dr. Bill Smithson and Wor. Bro. Harry Beaton, and all the members of my Mother Lodge, The Lodge of St. Oswald No. 1124, both past and present, with thanks for the confidence that made the writing of this book possible.

No, We're Not a Funny Bunch of People!

by Johnny Lancaster.

Foreword.

The purpose of my writing this book is, in my own modest way, to put a side of Masonry which has, to my knowledge, not been expounded. By this I refer to Masonry as seen from the stand-point of an ordinary member.

In Masonry it cannot be denied that we now have, and have had in the past many, famous and distinguished people as members.

Were any such person to have written this book it could be misconstrued that some ulterior motive lay behind the effort. My own position is far more commonplace. Apart from the fact that I have been in Masonry for almost a quarter of a century, I cannot make any claim to importance. From this viewpoint it is my intention to collate, for the reader, aspects of Masonry that have hitherto not been presented.

All too often Masons have received bad press. On many occasions this has been the result of a deliberate attempt to denigrate the movement, but many articles have been written with only a partial knowledge of the subject. The loser on every occasion has been Masonry as a whole and the overall picture has become distorted. Despite the many false accusations levelled at our organisation no-one has yet set out to put the record straight, particularly at grass roots level.

In this book I will attempt to show Masonry in its true light and to dispel some of the myths which surround our institution, as well as introducing some of the people, some well known, some not so well known, who are proud to be numbered among its members.

Contents.

No, We're Not a Funny Bunch of People!

Chapter: One.

The Secret Society.

Masonry is a secret society! In one short sentence we have thrust before us the greatest of all Masonic myths.

Nothing, in fact, could be further from the truth. Masonry is there for all to see and most Masonic Halls have a sign above their doors bearing a legend to that effect.

There is absolutely no secret about any person being a member. If any member were to be enquired of as to his membership there could be no reason for his denying his involvement. If the truth were known he would probably impart the knowledge with no small degree of pride.

In certain circles it has been put forward that such and such a person has not declared his membership of Masonry.

This observation is probably correct but, like so many other points, has been taken out of context. There can be no case for declaring one's involvement if a specific reason for doing so is not apparent.

Equally, one would not volunteer the fact that one was a member of the local golf, tennis or bowls club if there were not a pertinent reason one to do so. "Would you like a round of golf old chap?" "Yes, I'll go and get my tennis racquet!"

In the normal course of events, conversation follows set patterns, and if, in these patterns, any one subject is not broached there can be no sinister reason attributed to the fact that any information pertaining to that subject has been withheld or concealed.

In numerous instances this observation is borne out by fact that certain members of our institution have known each other for years before they suddenly realised that they were both members. Unless some common denominator triggers a reaction, knowledge of some aspects of one's personal life are not offered as relevant information.

It is quite conceivable that one might play golf with a fellow member for years without actually knowing how he earns his crust. Such information can be irrelevant when engaged in the frustrations of propelling a white globule over a vast distance into a hole of unseemly dimensions. "How many did you take there old chap?"

"Ten!"

"Oh well done. Your hole! By the way; I'm the entertainments manager on a Norwegian whaler!"

It does not work that way in golf and it does not work that way in Masonry either.

Knowledge on any given subject is sometimes difficult to come by in its simplest and most pragmatic form. One very prominent member of my local golf club was once asked. "How are you, Frank?"

To which he replied "mind your own business!"

Before leaving this one specific area it might, at this juncture, be worth recording that the kind of people who take an interest in organisations such as ours, seem either to join Masonry or Round Table. The fact that any person has or has not revealed his membership of Round Table has not, to my knowledge, ever been called into question, but this cannot reflect in any way on Round Table or its members but, whilst seeking to present Masonry in its true light, it must be acknowledged, that in certain quarters, we are regarded with total but not malevolent indifference.

One very hard working member of our local Round Table comes from a family who were all in Masonry. He has chosen to spend his leisure hours with the Table and has a track record of which he can be justly proud. Even now, in latter years, he chooses not to follow his forefathers but this is his choice and no-one would presume to question his calling.

Having dealt with the first great myth, let us now approach the second anomaly which is probably not as clear cut but which, nevertheless, is proffered by the antagonists as an unacceptable side of Masonry in general. "Masonry is a society with secrets!" Yes it is! But to understand this observation and, again, to put it into context, it is necessary to understand the history.

In early times, after the Dark Ages were over, the country was starting to be rebuilt. Building had, to all intents and purposes, ceased since the Roman occupation but now the ancient Masons were employed in the task of reconstruction. In the performance of this task they were peripatetic, completing a particular job or contract in one town before moving on to the next. As in present day construction there were different levels of skill attained and required. These levels of skill were rewarded by different levels of pay but, as they could neither read nor write, a method of communication was necessary to distinguish experience from inexperience. To achieve this a system of signs, symbols and passwords was devised.

A newly appointed mason was in those days, as now, known as an entered apprentice and there were a set of signs attributed to that stage or degree of proficiency. As the mason moved round the country he could give the proof of his ability by communicating these signs and receive the wages commensurate with his particular level of skill. The signs changed with each successive level of attainment until he became a Master Mason and was thus rewarded accordingly.

A parallel of these ancient customs practised by the operative masons of the past have been adopted by the speculative masons of today who form the Freemasons lodges which exist throughout the world.

As an interesting aside at this juncture, it is perhaps worthy of record that the ancient masons were in the habit of "autographing" their work by placing their own personal mark or sign on buildings which they had been instrumental in constructing. These marks are still in evidence today and form an integral part of our national heritage.

A typical example of this is the famous Imp in Lincoln Cathedral which can be seen by any visitor. It is carved into the stonework and is the "signature" of one of the masons involved in the construction of the building.

One of the most prevalent points on the subject of Masonry which, to my knowledge, has never been mooted or chronicled is that Freemasons not only have secrets which are not known to the outside world, they also have secrets from each other. This, however, does not make us twitchy with someone who knows more than we do and, whereas I'm not about to begin discussing the ifs and buts of the knowledge that I have personally acquired, I would assure the reader that anything I do know is not about to bring down any governments or start any revolutions.

Let us now trot out that old chestnut that is the subject of so many discussions and misunderstandings;

"Freemasons regard each other with special favour."

When you said you were going to put a Masonic
emblem on the car, I envisaged something
fractionally more discreet.

Yes! They probably do - but not for the simple rea that they are Freemasons! Freemasonry is a club and, as with any other club in the world, its members get to know one another well and, therefore, tend to seek each other's help in various situations.

In many instances the members have known each other long before they joined Freemasonry, particularly as one of the prerequisites for proposing anyone as a member is to have known that person well for quite some time.

Thus, to purport that any one situation is the result of two people merely being Freemasons is absolute nonsense, as is the observation that one or two bad apples will corrupt the whole institution.

Much capital has been made out of the fact that one or two of our members have transgressed from the paths of righteousness. This no-one will deny, but it must be emphasised that any such case is very rare indeed and culminates with that person being asked to resign.

If, because of such instances, the whole movement is to be taken to task, then the same must hold good for every other club and institution in the country.

By taking these various points and explaining them in context it may be hoped that the myth will, to a very great degree, be set aside. However, it cannot be denied that, by its own inbuilt reserve, Freemasonry has to a very great extent become a myth and nothing feeds off a myth like a myth. In like manner, on occasions the image of Masonry has been blown out of all proportion and, far from putting the record straight, Masonry and Masons in general have withdrawn into that reserve and allowed the accusers to have centre stage and the benefit of the spotlight.

It could be argued that the effect has been the same as St. George and the Dragon. The world at large now knows that dragons did not exist but were a legend born from arboreal snakes attacking people from trees. From this beginning were derived the stories of dragons and the image of the dragon in everyone's mind is the popular depiction of St. George slaying an enormous beast that was shown as being bigger than his horse.

So has the misconception been formed of Freemasonry. The misconception has been fuelled by those who, for whatever reason, sought to take issue. It is not my intention to use this book as a platform for debate, but one observation is perhaps worthy of being made.

In all the discussions and writings made up to this time, everything has been on the negative side. Nothing has been put forward to commend the institution. I would take just one example to illustrate my point.

The television series on the subject of Inspector Morse was undoubtedly a production of merit and founded on some excellent script writing. It was with sadness that I watched an episode which contained a disparaging reference to the Masons. It had no meaning. It did not present itself in context and had no relevance to the story in any way. It certainly had no relevance to any Masonic connection.

For my own part, I was just left wondering - "Why?"

In the following chapters I would like to introduce the reader to some of the people who not only make the whole thing tick, but to some of the many Masons who enjoy simply being members for the sake of being members.

At the end, the task will have been worth it if the reader is sympathetic when I say,

"No, We're Not a Funny Bunch of People!"

No, We're Not a Funny Bunch of People!

Chapter: Two.

Behind Closed Doors.

As was discussed in the opening chapter, there is a veil of mystery that enshrouds the Masonic world which gives rise to innocent speculation on the part of some, and licence for the generation of disquiet and unease on the part of others.

Because there is an area of Masonry which is not openly discussed, even among fellow Masons, the whole aspect of Masonry has assumed a cloak and dagger type of image which has allowed the generators of alarm and despondency to fan the flames of apprehension with consummate ease.

If the truth were known, and more to the point, told, a Masonic evening is an innocuous affair, providing an evening of leisure for the majority, an evening of satisfaction for those who are engaged in the administration, and an evening of social acceptance and general harmony for all concerned.

The overall events of the Masonic evening are not a secret. Any Masonic caterer or their staff, the majority of whom are ladies, would be able to impart this information as easily as the members themselves. The only information which is restricted is the knowledge of the various parts of the ceremonies themselves.

I have deliberately used the word restricted and not secret as, by definition, the knowledge is not a secret. It is merely restricted to those members who have already engaged themselves in that particular part of the degree.

An example of this is the Ceremony of Installation, or the ceremony where the new Master is installed, or placed, in the main chair of the Lodge for the forthcoming year.

When the moment arrives for the Installation itself, all present with the exception of those who have already passed through the Master's Chair are required to leave the lodge room, and only the Past Masters themselves are party to the proceedings. This does not in any shape or form give rise to consternation among those who were required to leave. Not only are the members quite happy to accept that this particular part of the knowledge is restricted, they are content to the extent that there is never any instance of a member soliciting the knowledge of a degree through which he has not passed.

Let us examine the events of a Masonic evening from beginning to end and dispel some of the suggestions that Masonry is more akin to the concepts of a Victorian melodrama than an evening in which the great majority of members can simply indulge in an evening of enjoyment in a social atmosphere.

The settings for these evenings are as diverse as they are colourful. They vary from the grandeur of purpose built lodges to the rural lodges which meet in a local village hall. Not every lodge has the good fortune to meet in a specifically appointed building. But, if the situation of the various lodges may differ, the internal layout of all lodges is, to all intents and purposes, the same.

Most lodges convene between the hours of 5 p.m. and 6 p.m. At the appointed hour the lodge is opened, the opening Ode is sung and then the Minutes of the previous meeting are read. The duties of recording of the Minutes and subsequently reading them are those of the Secretary. May I not let this moment pass without observing that some Secretaries can be lengthy and pedantic in the execution of this duty. On many occasions the reading of the Minutes has considerably shortened the Winter! Having said this let me also say that there are those Secretaries who do an excellent job, and one or two who turn the Minutes into something of an art form.

After the Minutes, various items are dealt with. Members of the Lodge who have been called to wander the pastures green in the Grand Lodge Above are remembered, visitors greeted and any relevant business is despatched.

The Ceremony itself then takes place. Because of the reasons I have already tabulated, I do not intend to analyse the Ceremonies themselves, and trust I will not be taken to task for not doing so. I hope by now that the reader will have begun to realise that the mystique of Masonry does not carry the heinous implications that some would read into it. Moreover, if we do not preserve the traditions of the Institution, then the substance of that Institution will, of necessity, lose a lot of its attraction and joining Freemasonry would become far less meaningful.

Which Ceremony takes place depends on the degree itself, but I will cover the points of the Masonic structure subsequently.

After the Ceremony any other business pertaining to the running of the Lodge is carried out, the Closing Ode is sung and the Lodge is closed. The members then repair to the bar.

There is generally an interval of some twenty minutes to half an hour between the Lodge closing and the dinner, or "Festive Board" as it is known in Masonic circles. This is the time of the evening when the whole lodge has a chance to mix and mingle and is an important period as far as the social side of Freemasonry is concerned. It is this time that is reduced if the proceedings fall victim to undue tardiness or a long-winded Secretary, it is thus necessary to remember that a balance in the events of the evening is highly desirable if the evening is to be enjoyed.

After the break, the members and their guests take their seats at the Festive Board where, after Grace has been said, dinner is served. The dinner is interspersed by various informal toasts. These having been despatched and the meal finished, the formal toasts begin, commencing with a musical version of Grace, and the singing of the National Anthem.

Continuing, after the Loyal Toast, there is a downward spiral of toasts beginning with that to The Grand Master, His Royal Highness, The Duke of Kent. The toasts go down through the various levels and offices until the penultimate toast of the evening, which is to the "Guests."

It is always incumbent on some visiting Brother to reply to this particular toast, and this having been achieved the final toast of the evening is that to "Distressed Brethren."

This done, the formalities are complete. Some of the members return, without further delay, to their homes, whilst others return to the bar. In latter years there has been a desire to comply with the drinking and driving regulations and this has resulted in a reluctance on the part of some to dally at the bar with the attitude of a bent elbow. For many people the car is the only means of transport home; the evenings of times past when it was pleasant to remain among friends and enjoy a pint or two whilst reflecting on the pleasures of the evening have, sadly, diminished in number.

It's gone awfully quiet in there. Either they've
put the subs up or somebody's suggested a
whip round.

Everything that I have recorded thus far in the chapter could have just as easily been related by any of the non-Masonic staff and employees who are engaged in the catering and administration of the Masonic world. There is no great secret! There is no great clandestine motive underlying the obvious.

If it is inferred that Masons are quietly eccentric, then we probably have to accede that we *are* possibly eccentric. But the gratification of that eccentricity does not sustain the suggestions and accusations levelled at the organisation that we indulge in activities which are beyond the pale and detrimental to the well being of our fellow mortals.

These accusations are not only unjust but unfair. The Masonic world is not the proverbial wolf in sheep's clothing. If the truth were but known and, more to the point, believed, Masonry motivates itself extensively for the good of mankind in general. One of the items of business undertaken by every lodge at every meeting is a collection in the cause of Charity. A subject on which I will expand elsewhere.

The Business for the Lodge on any given evening is set down on the "Summons" which is sent to members before every meeting. The Summons is not a secret document and can be read by all. I have had to generalise somewhat when recording the events of an evening as all evenings are not exactly the same; to understand this we must now examine the whole Masonic structure.

Masonry in England and Wales is controlled by The United Grand Lodge of England. This has its headquarters in Freemasons Hall which can be found in Great Queen Street in London. The head of this body is The Grand Master and, under Grand Lodge, England and Wales are split up into "Provinces" which roughly coincide with the Counties. The more populated areas are subdivided, as in the case of Lancashire, which is divided into the Provinces of East and West Lancashire. Each Province is controlled by a Provincial Grand Master, who presides over his own Provincial Grand Lodge.

Each Province is split into Lodges which, in turn, are controlled by their own Master. There is, however, a salient difference in the levels of mastership. The Grand Master has been in that office for twenty-five years, a Provincial Grand Master's term of office generally spans ten to fifteen years, but the Master of an individual Lodge gets one year and "That's your lot, dear boy!"

Occasionally a Lodge Master is in the Master's Chair for two years, but it's usually in extenuating circumstances such as someone dropping off the twig without giving due notice.

Under the Master, at all levels from the Grand Lodge downwards, come the other officers of the lodge. These include Wardens, Deacons, Secretaries, Treasurers and Stewards, all of whom have their various duties to perform.

In all there are thirty-three degrees in Freemasonry, the first three of which form the "Craft" or basic Masonry. The Grand Master is the Grand Master of the Craft and it is these first three degrees which form the foundation for all the others which are "Side Degrees."

It has been mentioned elsewhere that The Duke of Kent is not in fact the head man. This is totally incorrect. The Grand Master is indeed the Grand Master and is the head of Freemasonry in England and Wales. He is also the First Grand Principal of the Royal Arch Chapter which is the completion of the Third Degree. The Craft and Royal Arch Chapter run in tandem.

At this juncture I would like to spell out for the reader my own place in the scheme of things. I have done my first Three Degrees in the Craft and passed through the Master's Chair. I am in the Royal Arch Chapter and have similarly passed through the Chairs of that Degree. I am also in the "Mark" degree and the "Royal Ark Mariners" degree, but in these two degrees I am but a novice, not having been in either for any great length of time. There are many other degrees which I only know by name, thus comment on these would be pointless.

Before I am taken to task and informed that my lack of knowledge of the higher degrees invalidates the observations I have made, let me add that although I know nothing of the degrees themselves, I most certainly *do* know many of the members who make up their numbers. They include some of our most distinguished and respected Brethren.

The numerically higher Side Degrees are, in the main, patronised by the more mature members of Masonry because they can devote the time required of them. Amongst these members we could possibly locate a hard-core of enthusiasts to whom Masonry has become as much a vocation as an interest. They are the stalwarts, the Masonic Establishment at its best and its most dignified.

I have been privileged to meet a considerable number of these gentlemen. Their presence not only enhances the Masonic occasions for the ordinary members, it provides an aura which inspires the ambition of greater achievement. They provide a stimulant which motivates not only personal ideals, but epitomises the need and desirability of social harmony.

Let us now, having paid tribute to the achievements of the relatively few, return to the degrees on which the author *is* qualified to expound.

The Craft and Royal Arch Chapter are governed by "The Board of General Purposes" and the "Committee of General Purposes" respectively. These are names given to the main Masonic Committees which sit at Great Queen Street.

Membership of the craft is a prerequisite to joining any of the Side Degrees, which all have their own governing bodies and their own head men. Prince Michael of Kent is the Grand Master of the Mark degree, thus if the Duke of Kent were to attend a Mark meeting, he would hold an inferior rank to Prince Michael, but only in *that* degree. His situation would be similar in any of the other side degrees; however, in the overall scenario of Craft Masonry in England and Wales, he is most certainly, "The Boss."

Having looked at the top end of the spectrum, let us now consider the bottom. Once he has taken his First Degree, as with the ancient masons, the newly admitted member is known as an "Entered Apprentice." At the completion of the Second Degree his title is that of a "Fellow Craft." On concluding the Third Degree he becomes a "Master Mason," and this is where the rapid ascendancy ends, because the next stage of the ladder comes with the passage through the "Masters Chair." The first three degrees, depending on the lodge, may take a year to eighteen months, but in some lodges the attainment of the Master's Chair can take fifteen years. During this time it is necessary to pass from the lowest office of Steward, through the ranks of the lodge, to occupy the position to which most ambitious members aspire.

There are those who desire nothing more than to exist as ordinary members and go no further than the Third Degree. They may fulfil a useful purpose which does not require their occupying the position of Master, but generally speaking, most Masons are not content to languish in, what they consider, mediocrity. They very much want to get to the position of Master and enjoy the challenges which are synonymous with the accomplishment of holding that office.

By now the reader will appreciate the observation, "One can only get out of Freemasonry as much as one is willing to put into it."

There is an enormous amount of work to be put in over the years. There is a lot of "Mumbo Jumbo," or ritual, to be learned, and having learned and narrated the said "Mumbo Jumbo" to one's own and everyone else's satisfaction, there are all the side issues which must be dealt with. Who will organise any one event? A simple Carol Concert at Yuletide needs prearranging and can become the responsibility of any one given member. It is not expected that the Master and the Secretary should have to arrange every occasion on the agenda, and again, depending on the lodge and it's general attitude, the social calender of the lodge can be quite substantial.

By involving himself in the business of the lodge the Master Mason progresses through the various offices, is the incumbent Master of that lodge for one year and then enters the ranks of the Past Masters. After a passage of years he will be appointed to the Provincial Grand Lodge of his particular province and this is where the majority of members remain. There are, however, those members who do a considerable amount of work within the body of Masonry and contribute above and beyond the call of duty. It is these members who are promoted or appointed to the Grand Lodge, which is the greatest accolade which can be awarded, entitling that Brother to membership of what is, indeed, a very exclusive club.

Ireland has its own Grand Lodge, Scotland has its own Grand Lodge and each have their own individual Grand Masters, as does every other Grand Lodge in the world. The United States of America has fifty-one Grand Lodges and as with the Provinces in England and Wales, these roughly relate to the individual States themselves.

There are variations in detail from country to country but basic principles remain the same. Although there is a common bond between all Masons the world over, there is nothing sinister in that affiliation, with no great connivance taking place which is detrimental to the world in general.

In the writings on Masonry which would seek to discredit the institution, reference is made to the former P.2. Lodge in Italy. It has been implied that some very questionable characters have been members of this Lodge. I have no intention of discussing whether the allegations made regarding the activities of members of this Lodge are true or false, but let us for a moment *allow* those allegations to be true, and please note I only say *allow*. We are talking of one Lodge in thousands and, as with the individual members, the governing bodies cannot be held responsible for every undesirable occurrence which may take place. There is not a football captain alive who can be taken to task if one of the members of his team takes it upon himself to deposit the ball into his own net. The ball did not go into the net on the instructions of the captain, furthermore had the captain known of the forthcoming event, it is inevitable that he would have taken steps to prevent it.

Thus we have examined the structure of Masonry as a whole and also looked at the implications of membership for the individual. The doors are closed - Yes! - but they are not bolted. Anyone wishing to participate in Freemasonry has the chance to knock on those doors it being hoped that, on gaining admission, the newcomer will be gratified and pleased by the warm welcome which will inevitably await him.

No, We're Not a Funny Bunch of People!

Chapter: Three.

White Rabbits.

There was an occasion in my life when I was to witness a situation which was hilarious from the point-of-view of the bystander, somewhat tragic for the person involved, although there was nothing that could not be corrected the next time round, but, in the circumstances that we are discussing, strangely apposite.

I refer to an evening when, purely by coincidence, I witnessed a performance by a children's entertainer. Children are, sometimes, not the most sympathetic of audiences and many is the entertainer who has come off stage tearing his hair out and feeling that life, and children in particular, could possibly be a little kinder.

I once watched a show where the children spent the entire performance explaining to each other how each trick was done. Not only did they do it in extremely loud voices but their information was exceedingly accurate. By the end of forty five minutes the secrets of every routine had been analysed and the manipulator of magic was left wondering if there were not some other avenue of entertainment which could offer a more rewarding living.

The entertainer to whom I refer came on stage complete with top hat and cane - the very props with which to effect an entrance - and then placed them on a table.

He probably intended to make no further use of the former, but the children had noticed the hat and decided it must have significance.

The performance was now interjected by an enquiry from the third row.

"Where's the white rabbit?"

There was a pause, whilst a slightly puzzled performer in the mystic arts grappled with the implications of the question in his mind.

"What do you mean, white rabbit?"

"You've got a top hat! You must have a white rabbit!" replied his inquisitor.

"No. No. I don't have any rabbits. I don't have any rabbits at all. I'm sorry but there it is."

He now continued at the point at which he had left off, happy in his mind that one can sport a top hat without having a rabbit. Not so the children! Here was a conjurer! They knew he was a conjurer because that is how he had been introduced - and then there was the top hat. If he's a conjurer, and if he's got a top hat, then he must have a rabbit. This fellow must be taken to task!

"Go on. Show us the rabbit!"

This time the request came from the rear of the audience.

"Don't be mean!"

Perplexity was now manifesting itself on the face of the bunniless blackguard. Why had he ever used that top hat? He'd never used a rabbit in his act in his life and more to the point, before this particular set of pestilential kids had brought up the subject, he had never even considered the prospect.

"There is no rabbit," he said. A wan smile was on his face but he was feeling more as if in the role of the pantomime villain than that of the kindly "Children's Uncle."

He now continued his show as scripted and endeavoured to put the situation to the back of his mind.

"We want some rabbits!"

This time it was from the centre of the room.

"Yes. We want some rabbits! Go on. Show us some rabbits!"

The pack was in full cry! But, by now, what was demanded was not a cuddly bunny with big teeth and big ears, but the blood of this spoil-sport who had not produced what they were convinced should be in the hat.

The original idea had come from one or two of the children. The rest would probably never have even thought of the idea, let alone pressed the point, but now here was this unfortunate being with his back to the proverbial wall, and is it not much more fun to keep shouting for rabbits and witness the obvious discomfiture of a poor unfortunate than to sit placidly and watch the show which had been intended and rehearsed?

With no answer to offer, the luckless manipulator was now battling to continue his routine against an ever rising concerto of children's cries enquiring about rabbits.

All he could hear was "Rabbits." Could he show them something else to appease them? No! And, by now, any vestige of a conjuring show had been buried. The battle was lost! All his juvenile audience was interested in was the conjurer's skin. To continue was futile.

He went to the table and picked up the top hat and cane. With a mighty crash he brought the cane down on the table. He showed the inside of the hat to the audience and shouted at the top of his voice, "There are no bloody rabbits!!!"

He then stormed off the stage.

For a moment the children sat in silence. Then there was laughter. Then applause.

I haven't got a rabbit!

The children were delighted. What a wonderful evenings entertainment! Actually they had known all along that there were no rabbits around - well, they had been told that quite politely when they first enquired and there was no reason to disbelieve the man, but, more to the point, they had got him going and they had got him rattled. The fact that he was probably now sitting in his dressing room in a state of shock and moral indignation was not their concern. They had been shown where they might derive an alternative form of entertainment and had given the old fool a run for his money.

So it has happened with Freemasonry. One or two people have suggested there might be some rabbits around and they've sent everyone else in search of them.

They have actually been told before that there aren't any rabbits, but, as with the children and the conjurer, they have carried on shouting "Rabbits! Rabbits! Rabbits!" And, as with mud proverbially sticking, if someone keeps shouting, "Rabbits!" for long enough, there will be people who will believe that there are rabbits around.

Thus it is so with the great in-depth mystery which the sceptics try to attribute to Masonry. They would have us believe that there is something of which we are not aware. Something that cannot be seen. They have even hinted that there is something sinister within the constitution that is imperceptible from outside its confines; some great unknown force which weaves a magical spell on its members and bends their will to its behest.

This, I regret to say, is not only nonsense but the inference is speculative and could be damaging, if it were not so wildly wide of its mark.

Let us not deny however, that some of our members get even this wrong but, again, we have to blame the people in error rather than Masonry in general. There are people who have become disenchanted, sometimes through no fault of their own. They have worked hard and at the end of it all they have, perhaps, been overlooked. Some have had a bad personal experience or feel that they have been badly treated but, again, let me emphasise that the constitution would not be so set out for these things to happen.

From the ranks of the disenchanted there have been attempts to create "White Rabbits." One story that struck me, in a book on Masonry, was the instance of the man who had worked diligently within the confines of Masonry for some twenty years, during which time he had enjoyed his involvement and worked hard and long for the benefit of the Institution. It was then reported that, because of a conversation which he had with one of the hierarchy, his whole attitude changed and he decided that things "were not as they should be." He then withdrew his services having become disillusioned and disenchanted, to the extent that he was prepared to air his grievances to the outside world.

But, could it possibly have taken twenty years to find out the "ifs and buts" of any situation? I was told the "ifs and buts" of Masonry on the first night on which I joined. No secret was made of what is expected.

My own feeling is that this man expected some acknowledgement for his work which was not forthcoming and probably, with justification, he was greatly aggrieved. I speak with some authority on this subject as the same thing happened to me at one time; but I didn't blame the system. I blamed the people who got the system wrong.

Also reported in the same work was a complaint from a lady whose husband went to a Masonic meeting and returned home at 6 o'clock the following morning. This late arrival could have had little to do with Masonry for, all too often, I've been ushered through doors at 11.30 pm by a bleary eyed steward who has wanted nothing more than to go to bed. The party is usually all over by about 10.00 pm and nothing pertaining to Masonry could have lasted until 6.00 am.

All things considered though, one must always look on the bright-side. I've known ladies whose husbands never came home at all! And they weren't even Masons!

The human mind has a very fertile imagination and, when fed with a lot of irrelevant facts, it is not long before situations are blown out of all proportion, not by facts, but by pure supposition.

To illustrate the product of a fertile mind, I will relate a story told to me by a friend of mine who was an Inspector in the Hong-Kong Police.

Peter told me of the time when he was out in Hong-Kong and a friend arrived from London to visit him. Peter met his friend at the airport and, after the usual salutations and pleasantries had been exchanged, the friend told Peter how excited he was, never having been to Hong-Kong before and how much he had anticipated and looked forward to his visit.

He went on to say that he would like to have a really raunchy night and see night life to the full, indulge in an evening that would give full satisfaction to his lustful imagination and give him something to remember for the rest of his life.

Peter looked at his guest, paused, and then said, "Well it can be arranged, but it will be very expensive."

Undeterred, his guest replied, "That's absolutely no problem. Cost is irrelevant."

There was another pause. Peter said, "When I say expensive, I mean *very* expensive. What I'm saying is, it would cost a few thousand pounds, as I trust you would want me to come with you?"

There was now a look of apprehension on the face of our traveller. Having acknowledged that he would indeed like Peter to accompany him, he somewhat hesitatingly asked for an explanation.

"Well." said Peter. "If you want an evening such as you describing, you and I must get back on the plane and go to London. Having got to London we must then go to Soho where you will be able to have an evening such as you're describing. We have nothing out here in Hong-Kong which can even get near it!"

As with Peter's guest's concept of Hong-Kong, the concepts some people have of Freemasonry are distorted. Disdain has been shouted from the roof-tops and the mud has been thrown, some of it sticking on the faces of good and kindly people who should never have had to suffer the indignity of slanderous accusations. Furthermore, these unfortunates have been placed in the invidious position of having to defend, not only themselves, but the institution as a whole.

Should anyone enquire as to the presence of White Rabbits in the future, we would not expect our masters to reply in the same vein or with the same profanity as the conjuror, but possibly a more conservative notice on the main door of Freemason's Hall would benefit the situation:

"The Board of General Purposes regrets to announce that there are no White Rabbits in this building or any other Masonic building - but we would acknowledge that some of our Members do keep them as domestic pets!"

No, We're Not a Funny Bunch of People!

Chapter: Four.

The Conveyance before the Traction.

Much has been written about membership of certain Lodges and the implications have been that there are benefits to be derived from membership of them. It has also been suggested that connivance on a grand scale can occur if influential people are allowed to come together under a Masonic Banner.

This is a red herring of enormous proportions, as the truth of the matter is very simple. In the main, members join a particular lodge because they already know some of the membership thus, if they should wish to indulge in any matter of connivance, then the Lodge or its surroundings would offer no assistance in these matters, because there is no machinery within the confines of Masonry which could realise such hopes.

If it were to be that certain members wished to hatch some scurrilous plot, they would be well advised to find quarters far away from the Masonic world in which to gratify their impious designs. A Masonic Lodge is hardly a suitable venue.

Two Lodges in particular have been subject to close scrutiny - the Guildhall Lodge and the Manor of St. James Lodge, both of which meet in London.

The Guildhall Lodge is largely made up of City gentlemen amongst whom can be found a goodly number of members who are past Lord Mayors. The impression given is that, because all these people met in a Masonic Lodge, there is some underlying factor which cannot be perceived by an outsider. This again is rubbish for the simple reason that, if a number of City administrators, including a batch of ex-Mayors, wanted to assemble to engage in some devious business they certainly would not have to have a Lodge in which to meet. They could meet in Guildhall itself.

So vociferously are the arguments put forward, one could be forgiven for getting the impression that, if one were to join the Guildhall Lodge, one would be well on the way to becoming Lord Mayor of London.

The Manor of St. James Lodge was formed by the Police in London, its inception giving licence to another spate of literary police bashing. All the old chestnuts were brought out about the undesirable effect on the Police Force and how the public is almost put at risk by some supposedly corrupt motives.

I do not intend to dwell on this particular point as it is covered in another chapter of this book; I would only mention that the members who formed the Manor of St. James Lodge must, of necessity, already have known one another.

The advantages gained would have been purely social and could not have affected any status quo, nor had any detrimental effect on the Force itself.

Let us now address the aspect of corruption in town halls. Again, what the authors of despair have done is to find an instance of purported corruption which has occurred within the confines of local government and attempted to show that there was some kind of Masonic connection, inferring that the offenders had orchestrated their supposedly corrupt moves by means of an imaginary Masonic bond. However far one reads, it all remains supposition.

There isn't one piece of hard evidence that Masonry, or any Masonic influence, had any bearing on the cause or result in any shape or form.

I'd like a pint to take home please. I can hear the
music just as well in my lounge as I can in yours.

If, therefore, it would make life more bearable to the prophets of doom to discover an actual instance where one Brother had solicited the assistance of another in an extremity, I will oblige and provide an actual case history.

In the book to which I referred previously, was chronicled the story of the gentleman who had bought a public house with the idea of turning it into a musical venue. He fell foul of the local inhabitants on the grounds of noise nuisance and there was a campaign against continuing his licence. Eventually, it came to pass that his licence was revoked and the unfortunate entrepreneur came out of the whole thing in a poor way.

Again, the inference was that a Masonic conspiracy had contributed to his downfall, simply because some of the people who objected to the renewal of the licence were Masons. I have the greatest sympathy with an individual who finds himself in the situation as described. It does seem as if the world is against all aspects of one's existence and unhappily, in circumstances such as this, the licence is the difference between being in business and out of business.

Noise levels are a constant bone of contention in licensed premises and many is the licencee that has come to grief because of a surfeit of decibels, but, surfeit of decibels or not, there could be no reason for a Masonic conspiracy to oppose them. If a number of Masons were to band together to object to the continuance of a licence then they would be doing it as individuals and not specifically as Masons and there could be no reason to suppose otherwise.

As if to typify the assertion I have been making, it once befell to me to solicit the assistance of a Masonic Brother in similar circumstances to those which I have described. During one stage of my chequered existence,

I was the licencee of a club in the South of England. In similar manner, my licence was called into question by a small percentage of my surrounding neighbours.

By coincidence, one of my members was not only a fellow Mason and a fellow golfer, but was also, by vocation, an Environmental Health Officer, his department being responsible, along with the Police, for club licences.

Colin was quite well aware of the standards to which the club was run. As I often said, if it had been any quieter it would have been shut. I rang him up and asked for his assistance.

Let me here emphasise that the assistance I was asking for was in his capacity as an Environmental Health Officer and not as a Mason. I felt that this approach was not untoward as, on a previous occasion, Colin had seen fit to visit me in his official capacity, that visit having cost me the proverbial bomb, it having been necessary to upgrade various facilities and amenities within the club in order to comply with the dictates of Colin's department.

The reply I got from my local Council Official, golfing associate, Brother Mason and friend, left me absolutely flabbergasted. Colin told me that being a member of the club made it requisite for him to "declare an interest," and withdraw from the case.

It struck me as ludicrous that a Government Official can cost someone a small fortune in one set of circumstances but have to withdraw in times of difficulty, simply because of familiarity. Nevertheless, this was how the cookie crumbled. Colin was not involved in the subsequent investigation.

There can be no *Masonic* reason for wanting a public house shut-down. Let us not forget that our topers have got to have somewhere to quench their thirst.

For my own part, my friendship with a Masonic Brother was of no benefit to me in times of need. It was left to his fellow officers to determine that the case against me was invalid, thus negating some of the "all pals together, no matter the weather" attitude which the outside world seems to attribute to Masons.

So the attitude that Masons join particular lodges to gain advantage seems to lose some of its credibility.

A Mason's Mother Lodge is the Lodge into which he is first initiated. In my case this was the Lodge of St. Oswald No. 1124 in the Province of Shropshire, a Lodge which was, at that time, proud to number amongst its members the Deputy Provincial Grand Master, who was a great friend of my father. I joined St. Oswald's in 1969 at the age of twenty-six, primarily because my uncle was one of the members, and also because I had known many of the members for the greater part of my life. They didn't even bother to interview me.

I enjoyed my time in Shropshire. For some years I was invited to entertain on Installation evenings - an accolade that I did not fully appreciate until later years. I remember that they all used to watch Dick Parry-Jones, the Deputy. If he laughed - they all laughed!

My Father's Lodge was in Scotland, not that he was Scottish. By virtue of his profession it was a matter of convenience that he joined a lodge north of the border.

It is with sadness I record perhaps the greatest anomaly of my Masonic life. Because of our various peregrinations, my father and I always passed like the proverbial "ships in the night," and because of those circumstances I never, ever, attended a lodge with my father.

I joined my Sussex Lodge because a number of people from Butlin's Head Office were to be found amongst its members, people I had known for years. They closed Butlin's Head Office some years ago, so all my former friends have departed, but I am still very happy in the company of the rest of the members of the Lodge.

It would not be unfair to observe that, even after a member has joined a lodge, he is still very much judged on his own merit. There is no magic formula whereby anyone is accepted purely on face value. As with any profession, the basic qualification is only a beginning.

That man is a doctor. But is he a *good* doctor? - Is that man a *good* musician? - So we ask the question. - Is that man a *good* Mason? And also - is he a *good* man?

I trust I will be believed when I say that advantage cannot be gained without diligence. That diligence being as much for the welfare and well being of others as for oneself. Initial membership of a lodge, although gratifying, is only a transitory situation. That member is in a position to further himself, but only after much endeavour will this object be achieved. Merely to join *any* lodge is but the first step on a considerably high ladder.

Sometimes the conveyance is placed before the traction, but I trust my exposition on the reason for membership of a lodge will provide enlightenment for the outside world, dispel some of the myths and rumours regarding membership, and put the horse and cart firmly back in the right order.

No, We're Not a Funny Bunch of People!

A Policeman's Lot is not a Happy One.

When it comes to the police the antagonists of Masonry have had a field day. They've dragged up case after case where some unfortunate member of Her Majesty's Constabulary has gone over the precipice and hit the rocks at the bottom. Speculation has abounded that in every instance there has been some inherent aspect of Masonry which has prompted these undesirable examples and it has been inferred that Masonry itself has the effect of corrupting the Police Force.

Prospects of promotion have been called into question and it has even been hinted that unless certain members of the Force became Masons their very careers were never likely to "take off."

This is absolute nonsense and, although there have been documented cases where the subject taken to task has been a Mason, the connection with Masonry has been amplified by *inference*. There has never been a shred of evidence that Masonry, in any shape or form, has been instrumental in the misdemeanours of any individual.

There have been accusations of "cover-ups" within the Police because officers involved were Masons. One could not deny that evidence in these cases has been substantiated, but if one were to remove the smoke screen and look again at the problem objectively, then one would perceive that the "cover-ups" were perpetrated, not because the members involved were Masons, but because they were fellow officers.

In contrast, there is one detailed example on record where a Police Officer guilty of corruption endeavoured to find solace by virtue of the fact that he and his superior were Masons. It did him no good and his superior was instrumental in his downfall.

Masons in general are not very sympathetic when a Brother transgresses. Not only are we supposed to toe the line but we are certainly not expected to cause embarrassment to our fellow members. In all fields of Masonry, members find very short shrift if they are seen, in any shape or form, to be "bucking the system."

To bring the case against the Police into perspective, what we must do is examine the situation of the members of the Force as individuals, look into the reasons that people join Freemasonry, and finally explain the question so often put forward by the outside world "What is it that Freemasonry has to offer to it's members and what is this miraculous hold that keeps its members together?"

Because of bizarre circumstances in which members of the Constabulary find themselves, their reliance on each other is not only desirable but totally necessary. They are a community within the community performing a wholly necessary but largely thankless task. They are, therefore, drawn together by a common bond and are largely dependant on each other, not only for support at work, but for their social life, and it is because of this dependence on each other that Freemasonry is so popular with the Police.

Social activities are a matter of individual taste. One man's meat is another man's poison. And on this note let us explore the reasons why people join Masonry.

And if the Chief Constable doesn't win this
afternoon, you won't be going into the Chair of
the lodge next year, you'll be going straight back
to the Steward's bench.

There are two main reasons. They consider there may be advantages to being a member because of the folklore that has grown around the mystique, or more usually, the most common reason is that they are simply curious.

The first reason is certainly the most vaunted by the anti-brigade. It must be said that there is a lot to be gained from Freemasonry, but not in the way that is generally believed.

There are those who have put in a tremendous amount of work for the benefit of others and those others include a lot of people who are *not* Masons. From this they derive a lot of well earned satisfaction but there are no actual material benefits.

Likewise, it cannot be denied that there are those who join because they see a possible path to instant preferment, but disillusionment is not long in raising its ugly head. It must be said however, that even amongst this band of adventurers there are those who having joined because they felt they might advance themselves, have realised their mistake, settled down, accepted the system for what it is and have become excellent members.

On the downside, it is only fair to record that there are a smaller number of people who join for all the right reasons and with the very best of intentions but, sadly, find that it wasn't quite what they expected. This is no fault of either party and generally results in a gradual fading away or resignation. This syndrome is regrettable, but it does happen.

And so we come to curiosity. What is it that this movement has to offer? What incentive do these people have for dashing hither and thither with various bags and boxes clutched in their hands, and why does this camaraderie and bonhomie exist amongst its members? These are the questions the outside world asks and which I now endeavour to explain.

As I have already pointed out, in joining most institutions the applicant has a fixed idea in his head of what he is trying to achieve. In joining Freemasonry, however, nothing is certain until membership is actually attained. Even on the night of initiation the entire spectrum is not apparent to the newly admitted Mason. After admission it soon becomes evident that there are a lot more sides to it than meets the eye. It is because of its various facets that Masonry appeals to its members and generally speaking, there are some aspects which appeal to everybody.

Some are fascinated by the Ritual - or the "Mumbo Jumbo" as I have heard it referred to. Some like the secretarial side, some find themselves at home with the finances, the charities or some merely enjoy the company of people with whom they now have something in common.

There are the "knife and fork" Masons. These are the ones to whom the Festive Board (the dinner after Lodge) has the greatest attraction and then, as it has been documented elsewhere, we have our share of topers. However, I would stress that they were topers before they joined Masonry. If two or more members wish to get together after Lodge and have a booze-up, it can hardly be said to be the fault of the Board of General Purposes. Their objective could have been achieved in any hostelry duly licensed to sell the products of the hop, rye or grape.

Somewhere along the line most people who join Masonry find an affinity with something or somebody and having made this point let us now return to the upholders of law and order.

Accepting the fact that the Police, by vocation, live insular lives, then accepting the fact that there is in existence an institution within which they can find a common affinity, it naturally follows that the Police would gravitate towards such an institution.

In such a situation they are capable of filling their leisure hours in an environment in which they can feel at ease, feel that nothing is being asked of them and, more importantly, be in a situation where they are thought of as members of the Lodge rather than members of the Force.

As a matter of fact, on the occasions when they do something for the benefit of Masonry, they are always thanked.

No, We're Not a Funny Bunch of People!

Chapter: Six.

Dearly Beloved Brethren.

Religion as a subject is a natural minefield and before starting on this subject may I first say that I am in no way a theologian and that I would not be commenting on the subject through choice. However, as we Masons have been accused of having diverse religious motives, even to the extent of encroaching on the occult, then it necessarily befits the situation that I at least tabulate that which is, rather than that which might otherwise be left to the more than vivid imaginations of the enquiring minds.

The main bone of contention is that, in their prayers, Masons pray directly to God - or the "Great Architect of the Universe," as he is known in the Craft. This is done for the specific purpose of allowing men of all nations, colours and creeds to unite on common ground. I have been brought up in the Christian faith but, to a Muslim, the Great Architect takes the form of Allah, and so on and so forth.

The argument is put forward that because we Christians pray, in Masonic circles, directly to God we are denying Christ. This is tantamount to saying that, because we occasionally take the non-stop train from London to Glasgow, we consider that Birmingham doesn't exist. It has to be a totally laudable situation when men of different nationalities and callings can stand side by side and, for that period in time, unite in their ideals and beliefs. From my own point of view, it has never even occurred to me that my Masonic involvement should influence my views on Christianity.

With regard to Christianity in particular Dr. Barbara Thiering, who teaches in Sydney University's Divinity Department, has unleashed yet another bombshell for the world to ponder and for theologians to explain. I refer to her thesis concerning the relationship of Christ to Mary Magdalen. This point of view will no doubt be considered and may influence the thinking of some but it must be understood that, in mature minds, ideas of religion are individually formulated and new concepts and new ideas, although worthy of consideration, are somewhat transitory thus, after consideration, opinions revert to those which have already become established.

It must be said that the great majority of Masons accept Freemasonry on face value and do not analyse the implications of every detail. Suffice to say there is nothing that causes alarm and consternation to them and they are quite happy to go along with the system as it exists.

The initials R.N. which follow the good name of Michael Higham, the Grand Secretary, do not stand for Religious Notary but indicate that he has been driving a boat around the waters of the world in defence of the realm.

It is he who is at the sharp end of all the urticacious barbs which are hurled at the establishment by the disbelievers and jibers. Because he is not a cleric, it is perfectly understandable if some of the religious accusations levelled at our society require a modicum of research before an answer can be forthcoming.

Such must have been the case when we were practically accused of dealing in Satanic Rites. Some researchers went to great lengths to prove that one part of the Royal Arch Chapter Ceremony related, not to the Great Architect, but to the Devil. It was a long winded and highly improbable hypothesis, but it has to be said it totally wrong-footed Grand Lodge, not because it was true but because the mere fact that anyone could suggest it might conceivably be *thought* to be true.

Let us not forget that the great majority of the members who form Grand Lodge and sit on the Board of General Purposes are on a par with me when it comes to an in-depth knowledge of Divine affairs.

This accusation threw them into a flap, and it was decided to take a long, hard look at the point in question; we were not prepared to allow even the faintest suggestion that we were indulging in anything other than that we all believed to be references to the Almighty.

Hence a change to the Mumbo Jumbo. One of the accusations I have read is that Masons indulged in "blood-curdling oaths" and long-winded stultiloquence. But let us not forget that our ceremonies were formulated in the 17th Century when pen pushers were fond of blood, gore, thunder, lightning and never used one word when twenty would do. They loved to use the English language to its full extent and their writings were very flowery in their content.

Some writers are known for what they say and some for how they say it. Shakespeare was the supreme example of having the happy ability to combine both facets but let us not forget that if we wished to précis the soliloquy from Hamlet down to three or four sentences, it could be done, but it would no longer reflect the genius of that worthy man and, more to the point, it would lose all the entertainment value.

So it is with Masonic writings. Take away the trappings and with them goes the essence. The one example which conflicted with this viewpoint was Mystical Lecture in the Royal Arch Chapter Degree. This was the point in question and this was also the most ungainly part of the Masonic writings. Our masters therefore killed two birds with the same proverbial stone. They removed all semblances of anything which might be misconstrued and at the same time simplified one of the most mind-boggling pieces to confront the apprehensive Masons.

They were kind enough to achieve this before I reached the Chair in Chapter and may I here record my thanks, as I only had to trot-out the new version and was spared from the ordeal of ploughing through the original.

This said, let us reconsider the implications of oversimplification. If we were to simplify everything, to remove the inherent phraseology, to modernise everything so that we did everything as if it had been formulated in the 20th Century, we would completely destroy the fabric of Masonry. It would be tantamount to putting go-faster stripes, spoilers and a Comic Relief red nose on a Rolls Royce car.

Therefore, it might be most advantageous if Masonry were to close its ears to the wailings of the protesters, continue in the traditions which we have been proud to inherit, continue with the principals and tenets as they have been handed down and therefore retain the entertainment value. For it must be remembered that Masonry is to be enjoyed and, whilst I have been discussing some of the heavier points of Religion, let us also remember that the latter, too, can be enjoyed.

It is perhaps prudent to recall that the Good Lord made us in his own image. It therefore necessarily follows that God must have a sense of humour.

A lot of my encounters with Gentlemen of the Cloth have been by virtue of my playing the organ and I retain many valued memories from years gone by of my many friends from the Pulpit brigade. These gentlemen are not without their sense of humour and there are many occasions on which it is a pleasure to recollect.

One saga with its roots in and still related in Shropshire is that of the vicar who had a habit of calling in at the Local to ensure that the "Flock" were duly tended. He was at the bar one evening when one of the old boys came up a little the worse for wear and ordered another drink.

"Prudence, George," advocated the vicar, "Let us not forget that over-indulgence is the ticket to Hell!"

"I know that Vicar," came the comment. "But when I get there, I'll tell them I've enjoyed the journey!"

I have tried to negotiate the minefield that this particular subject can present but there is just one point that I would, in coming to the conclusion of this chapter, put forward.

The period with which the Craft (the first three degrees of Freemasonry) is concerned with is B.C. or the period covered by the Old Testament. It revolves round the building of King Solomon's Temple, the first Temple at Jerusalem to be built on Mount Moriah, the highest peak in a range of hills generally known as Mount Zion, and was completed in 1005 B.C. It would therefore, be somewhat anachronistic if the prayers in these Degrees were through Christ.

Some of the higher degrees are specifically Christian degrees so Masons certainly do not deny Christ in every aspect of their constitution. As has already been documented, I am not in a position to expound on these higher degrees as I am not a member of them thus am not qualified to pursue the matter further. However, one observation I can make without equivocation is that in

I know they've made you Master of the Lodge but
I do think that gavelling before the sermon on
Sunday was a little bit over the top.

all the years I have been in Masonry I have never personally encountered any member who was at variance with this particular point of faith.

Masons are all men of mature age who have had ample time to formulate their ideas on religion and whatever may be argued to the contrary, these ideas are a matter for the individual conscience; once that is clear then any man can find peace with himself and his beliefs.

I think it would only be fair to record that Masons offer up their prayers and sing their odes with sincerity and gusto.

They also sing "The Queen" at every meeting; and sing it as though they are proud to be British. For my own part, if the lightning strikes the organ one night, I'll know I've got it wrong - but we do our best.

On the subject of organs I think it would be but fair to record that the author has never been known for a "sotto voce" approach when it comes to music. My dear old friend of many years, Baz, has often observed that I only know two organ settings - Loud and Off!

After one Royal Arch Chapter Installation, at which I had been playing the organ, I was talking to the Deputy Grand Superintendent for Sussex on the telephone.

"Nice music the other night, John." He said. "Perhaps a bit loud!"

I said. "Derek, when I'm playing the Great Architect's music I like to feel that he can hear what I'm doing!"

Dearly Beloved Brethren. I hereby close this Chapter.

No, We're Not a Funny Bunch of People!

Chapter: Seven.

Don't Make Me Laugh.

It was night time in the jungle and it was very dark.

A little rabbit and a snake bumped into one another.

"Good Heavens!" said the snake, "What are you?"

"You'll have to guess," said the little rabbit.

So the snake felt the rabbit with it's tongue.

"You've got big ears, four paws, a big fluffy tail and you're all furry," said the snake, "You must be a little rabbit!"

"Correct," said the rabbit.

"Come on," said the snake, "Now it's your turn. You guess what I am."

So the little rabbit felt the snake.

"Oh," he said, "You've got a bald head, a down turned mouth, big staring eyes and a nasty frown! You must be a Director of Ceremonies!"

For those readers who are unfamiliar with the term I would explain that the Director of Ceremonies is the Masonic equivalent of a Master of Ceremonies or Theatrical Producer. It is his responsibility to ensure that all that occurs during a Masonic evening goes as smoothly as is possible. This can sometimes be a thankless task. There is an old Masonic adage which dictates that, if all goes well the Master will be duly congratulated. Should things go awry, blame the Director of Ceremonies!

In any stage-show, a successful evening culminates in the players doing their "Nodding donkey" routine to the applause of the audience. It is only in the case of failure that second thought is given to the role of the producer. So it is in many walks of life. Credit and blame are not apportioned. They are categorised.

There are those among the Masons, and I am not only referring to the Directors of Ceremonies who, without a doubt, have either lost their sense of humour or were never issued with one. They view life and Masonry as a crusade and do not allow themselves the pleasures that laughter can bring.

When our masters made a comment to the media that Freemasonry was "Fun" there were those who showed great consternation and indignation.

"Fun? It shouldn't be funny!"

Possibly "Fun" is the wrong word. What is intended is that a sense of humour and a sense of enjoyment should prevail to compliment the more serious side of the proceedings.

During my years of membership I have encountered one or two of the more pious types who would certainly have been well advised to dispel the clouds of gloom and doom, cast off the veil that type-cast them as professional mourners and allowed themselves the pleasure of "lightening up." Nothing is more poignant than that old saying, "Laugh and the world laughs with you. Cry and you'll cry alone," and although Freemasonry has its serious side, there is also ample opportunity to enjoy the lighter side of the meetings and to indulge one's self in the pleasures of humour in good company.

Before I'm taken to task on this issue may I stress that I am not referring to a "send up" in any way, shape or form. Neither am I advocating that anything which is vulgar should be acceptable. What I am inferring is that it is undesirable to bury ourselves in the Ritual and then sit through the Festive Board as though our shares had dropped.

It is a particular point made by the Provincial Grand Master for Sussex that masonry is to be enjoyed, a decree that is certainly borne out by his own personality. It is apparent that he enjoys every aspect of Masonry and confirms this whenever he has the opportunity to speak. He is easy of address and never loses the opportunity of conveying the humorous side of any subject to his listeners.

Throughout my years it has been my good fortune to know many laughter makers, and many of these can be counted amongst the ranks of Masons.

One great show-business character who was not only a Mason but also a member of the Grand Order of Water Rats, the show-business equivalent of the Freemasons, was Max Seymour. Max was one of those endearing personalities who knew everyone - and everyone knew Max! He was a member of the Vaudeville Golfing Society and was famous for playing five or six holes, excusing himself from the assembled company and returning to the bar.

The bar and scotch were the great loves of his life and he insisted on doing full justice to both - not only socially but, in his later years, he actually ran a club in South London.

The Vaudeville Golfing Society is not known for its charity when commenting on any of its members in the programme of the annual dinner. One year the programme announced that Max Seymour had, that year, given two pints of blood - the recipients were too inebriated to say "thanks!"

Max was eventually called to the Grand Lodge Above and, again, the events were duly recorded in the programme of the Society's annual dinner. The entry ran -

"It is with regret that we report the death of Past Captain Max Seymour. After the Service Max was cremated in accordance with his wishes - It took three days to put the fire out!"

Elsewhere I have conceded that, within the Masonic bodies, we do have our fair share of topers - indeed my own situation has, on occasion, been called into question! No-one, however, has a greater affinity with the product of the brewing trade than Masonic Brother Baz.

Baz is one of those very laid back characters who take life at a gentle pace, is not prepared to be rushed into anything and who's existence is complimented by an ever present pipe sustained between his teeth. This portable furnace is encouraged by a never ending supply of matches and is as much a feature of an evening in the watering-holes of England as is its passive owner. In fact, he is an authority on them, having spent a lifetime appraising their various merits. He enjoys their peculiar ambience with quiet satisfaction, maintaining a somewhat studious approach to his pleasures. He is not easily agitated, his placidity disturbed only when circumstances result in an empty glass being noisily rattled on the counter accompanied by him, enquiring of his fellow travellers, -

"Did I buy the last round?"

Baz was the Organist of a lodge to which I once belonged in London and Baz did indeed enjoy his evenings to the full. He is a Mason who is happy to go no further than the Masonic keyboard, not aspiring to any other vocation within Masonry other than providing musical accompaniment whilst pleasurably anticipating a further indulgence at the end of his labours.

Prior to a certain lodge night, Baz telephoned the Secretary to make his apologies as clients had invited him to a business lunch on the same day as the lodge meeting. He was uncertain of the time at which his luncheon would end and asked that I would play the organ in his stead.

But I had other duties that evening, thus I could not accede to Baz's request. In the circumstances a substitute Organist was engaged to play for the lodge.

Murphy's Law being what it is, the night before the lodge meeting, the substitute Organist proffered his apologies. Circumstances precluded him from being able to provide the music the following evening.

Baz was contacted on the "Alexander Graham," told of the course of events and asked if he would try to cut his luncheon appointment short in order to attend the Lodge. Baz agreed!

The next day, we duly assembled, the last person to arrive being Baz. His arrival was announced by a stentorian salutation from the far end of the corridor.

"Hello!"

This was followed by a raucous laugh. It was at once obvious that Baz's clients must have appreciated his past services and had offered him more than the odd half-pint and black coffee with which to wash down his lunch.

Baz was affable in the extreme and, although time was pressing, he insisted on greeting everyone individually in a most cordial manner, even enquiring if we would desire to join him for a further libation prior to the commencement of the proceedings.

His kind offers were tactfully declined and, with gentle persuasion, the would be philantropist was ushered to his seat at the instrument.

The organ, that evening, sounded like something of which Billy Smart, or any other fairground proprietor, would have been proud! Baz went at it full tilt. Subtlety was thrown to the wind, and a sense of irritation might have manifested itself amongst the members had it not been for the sheer enthusiasm with which Baz was playing. It was loud - yes! There was the occasional "Domino," or wrong note, but Baz's face bore a constant grin and if the music was loud to everyone else, there was an obvious outside mellowing effect on the organist himself. He enjoyed it to the full.

He carried on enjoying himself, for, when the lodge was over, Baz was one of the first at the bar. His afternoon had been interrupted by the requirement to fulfil his Masonic duties, but now he was intent on picking up where he had left off. For the next half hour he freely availed himself of the various items on offer before the Festive Board, which would be the second social repast during what was proving to be a most pleasurable day.

Dinner was announced. Baz contented himself with taking the remains of his pint along with him. He was, by now, in one of those moods when the entire world was at peace, every moment was to be savoured and troubles forgotten. Numbered among those with whom Baz was about to satisfy the inner man was myself. As was always my custom, I took my place at dinner next to my life-long friend.

Baz is one of those gregarious characters who is good company for any evening, but on this occasion he excelled himself. He chatted to one and all and was the proverbial life and soul of the party. The first part of the festivities, although pleasurable, passed without event.

Presently, I perceived that the Master was about to call for order as a prelude to some of the toasts which intersperse a Masonic evening. He had in his hand his gavel and was waving it around in a manner which indicated a sense of urgency and a wish to "get on with things." He now held the gavel aloft, but, before bringing it down, he turned to a waiter and said, "And please could I have some more bread!" He then brought his gavel down firmly on the table.

I was sitting between Baz and the Master and the next thing I heard from my left was.

"Catch."

All concerned now perceived a bread roll in orbit. It left the hand of the happy organist, described an absolutely perfect arc through the air, (Ballistics Incorporated could not have been more accurate) and landed in the hands of the Master who had been forced to drop the gavel in order to receive the incoming missile. A cricketer fielding at long off would have been proud of such a catch.

It was achieved with aplomb and dexterity, and was rewarded with a round of applause from the assembled gathering.

Baz laughed! The Master muttered something about a "Modicum of decorum" but he had got his bread, not as he had intended, but everyone had had the grace to see the funny side of the situation. It was one of those instances when one can look back and say "It shouldn't have happened - and we must try and make sure it doesn't happen again in that way - but it was funny!"

So one or two of our members enjoy a binge on occasions but let me stress it is not the system that is at fault. Generally speaking there is not a lot of harm done even when, on the odd occasion, eight and one pints are consumed.

Having said that, let me emphasise one very prevalent point. The people I know who like their tipple, and are Masons, very rarely exceed the norm on Masonic occasions. There simply is not the time available in which to indulge in excess and the dinner has an arresting effect on the intake of alcohol. It would be totally undesirable to finish the Masonic evenings with the entire lodge, or even the preponderance of the members of a lodge, in a state of temulance.

Thus a happy medium is desirable. Moderation is looked for when it comes to the intake of alcohol and tolerance is necessary to allow the lighter side of life to be appreciated.

Masonry can be enjoyed if humour is allowed its place and enjoyment can be achieved without detriment to the institution or its members. Life in general offers many opportunities for a smile on even the most serious subjects.

An undertaker moved into the house next door to a club which I frequent. One night I heard the manageress enquire of him, "If the place was now going to be piled high with boxes everywhere?"

During his professional duties Kevin, the undertaker, maintains a professional dignity which befits a person of his calling. Having known him for some time it has become evident that the caring attitude he evinces in the performance of these duties is not an act. He genuinely cares for the people for whom he performs his task. He shares their sorrows and does all he can to reduce their burdens and to relieve their sufferings. He becomes a pillar of support at a time when its needed most and, if that support is received with gratitude and appreciation, he enjoys the personal satisfaction of an ambition achieved and a vocation fulfilled.

In his private life his sense of humour manifests itself to the full, complementing the social company in which he finds himself. His title in the club is that of "Boxum n' Burnum."

One thing is absolutely certain. No Mason, or anyone else for that matter, is going to be sent to the Grand Lodge Below for having a sense of humour. It is a tonic and those who are capable of brightening the lives of their fellow Masons and fellow human beings are engaged in one of the greatest charities of all.

Although the chapter begins with a reference to the Director of Ceremonies let me make it clear that not every Director of Ceremonies is lugubrious. One does not have to be in that particular office or indeed in any office at all to qualify as a party pooper. But before I finish this part of my observations, may I emphasise that, in Masonry, the party poopers are very much in the minority. Most people, no matter what their office or calling, have a sense of enjoyment and in common with their fellow human beings, share a wish to further that enjoyment.

Man is the only animal that is capable of laughing and crying as he is the only one which can differentiate between the way things are and the way things might have been. By making full use of this capability, we should be able not only to enhance our own existence, but to gladden the lives of everyone surrounding us. Not many people would deny that one of the most gratifying experience of all is a given set of circumstances,

Our Director of Ceremonies does have a
somewhat unique approach.

culminating in the realisation of humour, thus providing the opportunity for the inhabitants of this planet to have a damn good laugh!

No, We're Not a Funny Bunch of People!

Chapter: Eight.

The Masonic Foundations.

Every organisation in the world has foundations and a goodly part of the Masonic foundations are nothing whatsoever to do with the concrete which supports the Grand Lodge at Great Queen Street. They are born of the support given to the members by their ladies.

The fair sex play a large part in the social life of any Lodge, the highlight being the year in which their other half becomes the Master of the Lodge.

The term "highlight" could be fractionally incorrect in this context. It might be more accurate to say highpoint, for, to be fair, some ladies do view the prospect of this year with apprehension. They don't *all* relish the prospect of rising to speak at the annual Ladies Night.

Having said this, it is also true to say that, having negotiated this daunting hurdle, most ladies are able to reflect with pleasure and more often than not, a degree of satisfaction on their year as "Mistress of the Lodge" - as I once heard it described.

As with their male counterparts there are those ladies who contribute more to the social side of events than others, whilst there are some who are content merely to attend the yearly binge and subsequently play the part of an interested consort. There are also instances in which ladies pick their husbands up from lodge and in so doing, join the members for a drink in the bar afterwards. Thus they are well known to the greater part of the membership and become acquainted on a regular basis. Much to their satisfaction.

I have read a lot of twaddle on the subject of "Masonic Widows!" As the average lodge meets only six times a year this can hardly give rise to alarm and despondency on the part of the wives of the rank and file Masons.

As with every club or institution there are those members who devote a greater proportion of their leisure hours to Masonry than others. They become, for whatever reason, more interested in the subject and that which motivates the members, yet, in the main, an equilibrium is achieved.

If, to take the matter to the extreme, a member were to go absolutely overboard and indulge in attending meetings six nights in a week, against the wishes of his wife and family, it would not be the fault of Masonry itself. There is a balance which is not only desirable, but which should be maintained.

If a child becomes grossly obese and overweight it does not befit the situation to have a parent lob a brick through a window of the local supermarket. Supermarkets having set up their stalls to provide a balanced and advantageous diet and no supplier can be taken to task if that which is provided is indulged to excess.

Let us not deny that there are members who attend lodges very frequently through the winter months. There are those Masons who are involved, not only in the craft degrees, but also the side degrees. This involvement does demand a great deal of time in the evenings but it must be appreciated that these members are usually retired or well on the way to retirement. They have, therefore, spent the greater part of the day in the company of their wives and, generally speaking, the "Old boys" depart pretty smartly when the proceedings have finished. It is usually the younger crowd that stay behind to partake of a single for the highway.

The hierarchy, as a rule, make a point of fulfilling only their official engagements. Because of the demand on their time, they tend not to visit lodges on a purely social basis, but are more likely to adhere to the schedule of events as dictated by its demands.

To enable me to make this observation clearer to the non-Masonic reader let me clarify the point in question: As stated in the chapter entitled "Behind Closed Doors," every Province has a Provincial Grand Master. He will have a Deputy and a number of Assistant Provincial Grand Masters. In Sussex there are four Assistant Provincial Grand Masters.

It is the practice for every Installation meeting, or the evening a new Master takes his place, to be attended by an official representative from the Province. Thus the Provincial Grand Master, his Deputy or one of the Assistant Provincial Grand Masters will be present. At the present time Sussex has 171 Lodges, all of which have an annual Installation Ceremony. In addition to an official attendance at each of these, there are other functions that require official representatives to be present. The time required to fulfil these obligations does not leave much latitude for extra mural activity. Thus the members of the higher echelons are not often encountered, on a purely social basis, away from their own lodge.

A friend of mine was recently appointed to the position of Assistant Provincial Grand Master and, on receiving his appointment, Don immediately declined all further social invitations. To revert to the subject in hand - that of the ladies, Peggy, his wife, is seen at every possible social event and is very much the power behind the throne when playing her supporting role. Far from regarding herself as a Masonic widow, Peggy is proud of her husband's achievements and derives great pleasure from her involvement with the Masonic movement as a whole.

Because of the common interest, great friendships are generated between some of the ladies and, far from experiencing a negative influence from their Masonic associations, many of the ladies regard them as a vehicle for enhancing their social activities and the spectrum of their own lives.

Suggestions have been made elsewhere that there are ladies who are not happy with their Masonic situation in life. One volume, available for scrutiny, devotes an entire chapter to the writings of ladies who lay the blame on Masonry for their personal unhappiness, maintaining that their husband's involvement in Masonry had been a principal cause of it.

It is a sad fact that some people, and I am no longer talking solely of women but the men as well, tend to blame *anything*, not only Masonry but almost anything for the vicissitudes in their lives. Who has not said? "It's not my fault." It is so much easier to blame outside influences.

If a gentleman is prone to extend his period of occupation at his local hostelry, that is hardly the fault of the establishment or it's proprietor. Such instances are individual and each must be judged accordingly. On that basis, if a member spends more time than may be thought desirable in his Masonic activities it is not the fault of Masonry, as such.

At this juncture there is one point which must be conceded, not only to the ladies, but to all disgruntled parties. There *are* instances on record where the members *have* kept their wives at arms length when it comes to the subject of Freemasonry. This unfortunate scenario is not a product of the system. It arises because of the veil of secrecy which certain members seek to establish for reasons which are very much their own.

Sharon, the wife of a good friend of mine was a victim of just this type of syndrome. Purely because Mark was under the impression that he *should not* say anything to his wife, she was kept in ignorance of Masonry to a very great extent and consequently felt excluded.

By coincidence, Sharon's father had some very strange ideas on the subject. He had been under the impression that the original Masons were all illegitimate sons of Charles the First and he was opposed to the whole concept. Having read the contents of this chapter and realigned her own thinking, Sharon observed that she wished her father could have read the script as she was convinced that, in the light of the information that it offered, he would have totally changed his attitude.

If, through reading this work, there are any other ladies who enjoy a greater peace of mind in consequence, the effort will have been amply rewarded.

Let me re-emphasise the point that many members do not intend to give the wrong impression; very simply, they are not sure what should be divulged and therefore have said nothing. There is nothing clandestine in their motives but their lack of communication has been the generator of ill will.

Even having read and digested the salient points of this chapter there may be ladies who still feel rebuffed and consider themselves to be "Masonic Widows." It is to be hoped that their numbers are small and that sympathy is not lacking for their situation. However it can be mooted, without equivocating, that the plight of these ladies is nothing in comparison to that of a "Golf Widow."

Of course, he *will,* remember it's our anniversary
when he gets to lodge - I've changed his Masonic
apron for a nice pink one with flowers on, and
his white Masonic gloves for yellow ones of the
household variety!

"Golf Widows" really *do* exist. As I have said, a lodge usually meets six times a year, The golf courses of the world are open from dawn to dusk, three hundred and sixty five days a year and, at the majority of courses, the nineteenth-hole is open even when the only illumination for the previous eighteen holes is provided by the moon.

A Masonic evening lasts approximately four hours. A visit to the golf club can last all day - and most of the night as well. There are golfers who play practically every day of the week. They spend four hours on the course and then another four in the bar talking about it. This can have a mollifying effect as a missed putt of eighteen inches can get six inches longer with each ensuing pint.

One lady told me that she thought a series of tents around the first tee to act as temporary dormitories would suit her husband's requirements. Another told me her husband only came home to sleep, sometimes eat, and make sure he could still recognise the children.

Fishing widows are even worse off. Their husbands are literally out all night, and sometimes camp beside a lake for a week at a time, purely to fish. By comparison Masonic widows and, for that matter, the golfing widows, are in paradise. Solitude is enjoyed by some and endured by many. Those words of solace "I am never less alone than when alone" may be music to the ears of fishermen, but on their wives falls the burden of loneliness. This I merely quote. Let it not be stated that I set myself up as the judge and jury of the casters of hook and line. To each his own, my comments being advisory rather than condemnations.

Whilst professing my own indifference to unknown pastimes let me add the rider that it would also seem unfair for unknowing people to make harsh comments on the subject of Freemasonry when their observations can only be made from a stand-point which is, to say the least, peripheral.

Having mentioned "indifference," it would be appropriate to comment that it is not an attitude with which Masonic wives are viewed. In golf clubs male chauvinism still manifests itself to a very great extent and the lady members are frequently the butt of humour and the objects of derision.

Frank does have particularly strong views in this area. His definition of a ladies' four-ball is "Four people talking and no-one listening."

By comparison, Masonic ladies are positively revered; they are invited to all the social gatherings and even the apprehension attributed to the speech required of them can be overcome.

The ladies' occasions are enjoyed by all and are the end products of lengthy and meticulous organisation on the part of the more industrious members of the fraternity. The ladies play their parts to the full and duly complement the air of festivity. Let us not, however, suggest that Masonic ladies are "pure as driven snow" and thus to be set aside from other ladies. They have their quirks and traits and these are not dissipated by entanglement with a Masonic brother, or by the prospect of a Masonic knees-up.

Ladies, in whatever circumstances they may find themselves, tend to convey their thoughts, moods and the reasons for their apprehensions. This holds good in Masonic circles as it does in all others.

I was seated next to a very grandiose lady at the annual Ladies Night gathering of one of the Sussex Lodges. The evening was convivial and the company most cordial. Everything was running very smoothly but my dining companion was in a devilish frame of mind. She wanted everything analysed and an inquisition held on everyone present.

The meal was interspersed by various observations. Everyone in the room and whatever motivated them was investigated. The ladies coiffeurs were categorised, their dressmakers appraised and the value of their jewelry estimated. Nor did the gentlemen go without mention - no-one escaped - although the evening proved enlightening, illuminating and entertaining.

At every Masonic ladies night it is the custom for the ladies to receive a present. When the moment of this offering arrived my friend looked at the wrapping. She said,

"I'm not going to open it! I'm not going to open it! - Well, alright I will."

She examined the basic contents with an air of disdain and then, with an air of dismay said,

"Good heavens! They've written on it! I won't even be able to give it away!"

Ladies do have their moments which are beyond the comprehension of the nonplussed males, although these are usually transitory and pass on to be items of memory. In all walks of life men are grateful for the support given to them by their ladies and this is no more so than in the Masonic world. Masonry at large would be remorseful if any of the ladies were unjustly treated or felt put out or neglected because of their husbands activities.

All singular activities result in isolation for any given period of recreation, though the Masonic activities require far less than the other examples I have mentioned. Nevertheless, there is a tale of woe of a Mason and his lady which will confirm our Masonic brothers *do* occasionally fall from grace. - With the slight difference that the event to be mentioned was not actually a Masonic function.

Gerry and his wife were giving a dinner party at their house. Having made all necessary arrangements for the evening, Gerry departed his residence in the morning to see to various matters which demanded his attention.

His good lady did all required of her, and as the evening approached, everything was in place for the anticipated arrival of the quests. As with every dinner party, the lady was the mainstay of the operation. The male's is but a supporting role in these affairs. All was ready when the first of the guests knocked on the door. But there was no sign of Gerry!

Our abandoned lady now began the process of receiving the quests at the same time explaining that it had fallen on her to welcome them in a singular capacity. The whereabouts of her husband were unknown.

The last two guests announced their arrival by means of the door bell. Our lady, still without her consort and by now perplexed, irritated and indignant, answered the door. She welcomed the final couple and told them why she was so upset, finishing with, "and I've no idea where Gerry is!"

"Oh darling!" gushed the incoming lady. "We did wonder! He's asleep in that delightful hydrangea bush you have just inside the front gate!"

The evening was cancelled! This saga was recounted many times in Gerry's neck of the woods - not least to me. However, one always wonders if such a story is purely factual or has been embellished by the enthusiastic narrator.

It was some years later that I dined with Gerry at Lodge and asked him if the story were actually true. Gerry's eyes and forehead first rose, then his features reflected the man's resignation. He looked at me in the manner of a penitent with a painful memory and said, "Yerss."

Exception does not prove the rule and although there are those acknowledged instances of transgression by members of our fraternity, they do not and can not reflect on the body of Masonry in its entirety. We would thank the ladies for their indulgence. Without them not only would we not exist, we would be incomplete. They provide life and then give that life substance and meaning. Behind every great man......

My own personal recollections are endless and I can only reflect with gratitude and add my thanks to the ladies for the help, comfort and solace that I have received throughout my years - And the laughs! So many times are moments of mirth prompted by situations contrived by the ladies' involvement, situations that are unique and a pleasure to remember. These extracts from life would fill a volume all on their own but I will conclude this chapter with just one example which must go down in history as one of the all time classics.

At the end the Cynthia Payne trial the Judge requested the Foreman of the Jury to give the verdict. Having been party to a case of scandal, which was as entertaining as it was controversial, the gentleman rose and replied.

"We find the defendant Not Guilty M'Lord - but we'd dearly love to hear the evidence again!"

To ladies everywhere - our felicitations - and thank you.

No, We're Not a Funny Bunch of People!

Chapter: Nine

She ain't heavy, She's my Brother.

The song recorded by the Hollies in the 1960's is strangely apposite to Masonry, and had the requirements of Masonic music necessitated a Blues feel along with a strong off-beat, it could conceivably have become the Masonic anthem. Latterly, it has been used by the advertising media as an encouragement to topers, both Masonic and non-Masonic, to consume lighter coloured beer in ever increasing quantities. This served the dual purpose of raising the revenue of the producers of the golden liquid, and to give the song a second lease of life. Nothing, musically, was lost in the exercise.

By slightly altering the original title, and thus changing the gender, we introduce a group of people who are not as widely publicised as their male counterparts, I refer to the Order of Women's Freemasons.

Although the title of this chapter may imply that there is a connection between these ladies and the United Grand Lodge of England, the strange truth of the matter is that there is not. Not only are they unconnected, they are not officially recognised by the men. We know of their existence, we know they are there, we know what they do - but that is as far as it goes. The Order of Women's Freemasons are a law unto themselves.

I make this statement in its fundamental form for, although they are totally self-governing, one of their overriding concerns is that they should not cause any embarrassment to the male Masons. They go about their business in an unobtrusive manner, and happily, have not been subjected to the enquiring minds of the investigative media to the same extent as those of us who come under The Duke of Kent's guidance.

As we have a Grand Master, so do they with the salient difference that, of necessity, their Grand Master is a lady. The structure is exactly the same as that in male Masonry save that they have two Grand Lodges which permeate down through Provinces to individual lodges, the titles of the incumbents of the various offices being the same as ours.

The ladies refer to each other as "Brother." This may seem strange, until one remembers that a male nurse can become a "Sister." Anomalies exist in all walks of life and most people are content to ignore idiosyncrasies in others if those idiosyncrasies do not affect them personally. The mode of operation of the ladies is similar to that of the male bastions with the exception that there is no Festive Board after an ordinary meeting. Only an Installation Ceremony is followed by an indulgence in gastronomic delights. Their dress is very formal, a long black skirt being the order of the day.

The Order of Women's Freemasons has been in existence since 1908. It was then that they obtained the knowledge of the "Why's and Wherefores" from two reverend gentlemen and the ladies have combined their knowledge of Masonry with the accompanying social pleasures ever since.

The headquarters of their organisation is in London and, as with the constitutions governed from Freemason's Hall, the influence of the ladies' hierarchy in London permeates to the four quarters of the globe.

Despite all the similarities and mutual interest it must appear totally paradoxical that the two organisations do not officially recognise one another, but the simple fact of the matter is that they don't. Socially, the ladies entertain their gentlemen in a similar manner to us but, although there are male Masons married to lady Masons, the Masonic activities of the espoused are never mixed. They remain totally separate.

There may be those who read this chapter who did not previously know of the existence of lady Masons. Their existence is not as much publicised as their counterparts but, as with us, they are not a secret society.

In 1992, The Order of Women's Freemasons were the subject of an article in the magazine of a Sunday newspaper. The report was purely factual, but although the author did not set out to discredit the ladies in any shape or form, it was felt that the subject matter itself gave licence to a hint of underlying sarcasm. The sarcasm may not have been intended, but to some readers, particularly the ladies themselves, the inference was there.

It was the accompanying photograph from which there were no favours to be extracted. Instead of the desirable vision of smiling faces, the ladies were depicted in a state of unnatural solemnity. Solemnity which did not compliment them, or the subject matter in hand. Had one wished to place a caption underneath the photograph it would have read, "Caught on the 'op!"

It is far easier to portray the aspects of any subject in a poor light than in a good one. Happily, most photographs of the Duke of Kent give rise to the assumption that he has just enjoyed the winning shot at Wimbledon. I trust the reader will recall my observations in the chapter, "Don't make me laugh!"

Emancipation has changed the structure and the dictates of society in many ways. Barriers have been systematically removed and the world has enjoyed a

The Lady Masons are meeting tonight - it's so
much more refined. The way some of the men
use the gavel makes the proceedings sound like a
second-hand car auction.

greater degree of tolerance in consequence of change. Despite all these changes, the barriers of English Masonry remain. East is East and West is West. Men are men and ladies are ladies.

Maybe, one day, there will be recognition, but it will hardly be in the foreseeable future. It is an unusually unique situation that two organisations have similar aims, ideals and ideas and yet do not share their experience. The basic reasons for this situation undoubtedly lie in the fact that the respective constitutions would not permit any such latitude and, therefore, a mutual respect at a distance must take the place of more formal détente.

Times do change; let us not forget that it was only in recent years that, assuming membership to have been achieved, Mrs. Thatcher, the Prime Minister of the United Kingdom would not have been permitted to attend a Masonic meeting in Freemason's Hall.

Should change be achieved, and if it were ever to occur that the ladies were to invite a male Mason to one of their meetings, it could not be denied that a new frontier would have been reached. Supposition on the consequences is a matter for the individual mind, but one would be forgiven for indulging in a modest amount of conjecture as to who might get the first invitation.

No, We're Not a Funny Bunch of People!

Chapter: Ten.

Hands Across the Sea.

The members of the Masonic Brotherhood who have never actually wielded a trowel, or conjoined the contents of a bag of cement with sand and water, are known as "Accepted" or "Speculative" Masons. There are no actual building qualifications necessary for a member to find himself ensconced in membership, and it could be accurately assumed that there are those members who, given a real level or a plumb-rule, would be totally mystified as where, profitably, to situate them.

Speculative Masonry had its origins in Great Britain, but the rest of the world rapidly queued up for a bang on the drum. The United Grand Lodge of England was formed in 1717 and remains the first and foremost of all such Lodges. Masonry spread across the Continent, France forming its Grand Lodge in 1725, Spain in 1729 and so on. Masonry gradually spread across Europe and the Globe.

All countries have indigenous traditions which are peculiar to themselves and, in certain cases, areas within a country have their own especial quirks and traits. In England it is the home of the former Slave Trade, Bristol, which houses the greatest deviations from the norm. Things occur Masonically on the banks of the Avon which do not occur in any other part of Her Majesty's realm. How such deviations start is not always clear. The query of a visiting Mason as to why certain things are done in certain ways is usually greeted with the response - "We've always done it that way!" - and that's the end of that conversation! The spread of Masonry to the English speaking countries was a natural progression, and the existence of Masonry in these areas is well documented. Its influence also spread into South America where Masonry flourishes in abundance.

In some countries lodges exist miles from anywhere, the enthusiastic Mason having a route march as a prelude to his fraternal associations. Masons the world over unite in common bond, even if the circumstances in which they meet tend to differ. Some settings are very basic and the numbers attending small. Other settings are more opulent and the gatherings larger in number, and, that said, the moment has come when we will look at Masonry in its most prolific form. To do this we must turn our attention to the land of superlatives, whose citizens are used to doing everything on a grand scale; the land which is home to three and a half million Masons, and the land in which everything is reputedly the "biggest and the best."

The United States of America has taken Masonry to its heart, approaching the subject with an openness which is not apparent elsewhere. Whereas in most countries there is an inhibitive reserve surrounding the subject, this is not the case in Uncle Sam's fair land. There the Masonic Lodges are illuminated, in some instances, with flashing neon signs, Masonic items of clothing are seen in abundance, even car number plates have Masonic emblems, and the Masonic brethren of America think nothing of joining in local carnival processions, adding joviality and conviviality to any given occasion. Englishmen are known for their natural reserve and there will be those who read this information who would regard any such demonstrative behaviour with despondency and alarm. Yet the attitude of the Americans could well be considered as a lesson to us all because, as I have already discussed, there is a mystique about our existence which could well do with being kicked into touch; if we were to adopt a more open attitude, our institution would, probably, be better served.

In Britain, Masonry evolved long after the formation of the Country's political evolution. In America the two ran side by side.

It was in 1774 that Britain and America had their little disagreement, which culminated in Britain losing its most valuable colony. This all came about because Britain was trying to get money out of the Americans. Britain lost the punch-up - and America - and from my understanding of history nothing was achieved on behalf of Britain as we have been trying to get money out the Americans ever since.

Although it was the matter of Stamp Duty which resulted in us taking issue with our colonial cousins - or them taking issue with us, whichever way one looks at it - it was the Boston Tea Party which was to go down in history as the flashpoint of the fracas.

In this momentous event, Masonic involvement cannot be denied, as it was the Brethren of the Lodge of St. Andrews, which met at the Green Dragon Tavern in Boston, who actually dressed up as Red-Indians and physically dumped the dried leaves in the harbour.

The reason they assigned for this unfriendly visit was, apparently, to "see if tea would mix with salt water", - although the reason for the choice of costume is not abundantly clear. I would assure the reader that there is nothing within the Masonic dictates which would necessitate the members dressing up in hide and feathers to perform any of our past or present ceremonies.

I am also happy to record that I cannot discover any such instance of the Masonic topers dumping any of their beverages in the sea - that is to say, at least, not until they had first been recycled.

After the dissolution of constitutional ties with Britain, America also began the process of controlling its own destiny Masonically. The Grand Lodges of Massachusetts and South Carolina were formed in 1777, followed by Virginia in 1778. The other States followed suit, the last being formed in Oklahoma in 1892, until there existed the fifty-one Grand Lodges which make up the foundation of Masonry as America knows it today. Before these events, all Masonry in America had been controlled from Britain.

Masonry was in existence in America from the time of the Pilgrim Fathers, playing its part in the early American history, although it was not until 1733 the Henry Price was deputized as Provincial Grand Master of New England by the Grand Lodge of England. He has been attributed with the title, "The Father of American Freemasonry" and it was he who issued a warrant to the first lodge of Boston, later known as St. John's Lodge No. 1.

There were, doubtless, early Americans who were grateful for their Masonic affiliations. One such must have been the scout, Israel Putnam when, during the French and Indian War in 1758 he was captured by Indians. These somewhat unfeeling beings were preparing his premature dispatch to the Grand Lodge Above by way of tying him to a tree and cremating him in a state of consciousness. It was only when a French Officer, Count de Molang, realised that friend Putnam was, indeed, a fellow Mason, that he put an end to this impious design and extinguished the flames.

Gratitude was not long in being evinced. The following year Molang Lodge was formed in honour of the bearer of its name.

There may be those non Masonic persons reading this who will suffer a feeling of indignation that favouritism was shown on behalf of the good Count because his adversary was a Mason. May I invite them to reflect on the positive, rather than the negative, side of this situation.

If all disputes were settled in the amicable manner that Masonry dictates they should be, incidents such as the prospective barbecuing of poor old Putnam would never occur. Arguments would be settled by a dignified withdrawal and subsequent silence. Furthermore, in this case at least, the environmentalists would not have to worry about the destruction of trees in the process.

Many people in early America used Masonry as a moral yardstick. It was quoted that "Masonry taught men to live orderly, upright lives before God. In doing this a clear corrective was provided to the confusion besetting society."

Latterly, Theodore Roosevelt said, "Masonry achieved that equality promised but imperfectly achieved in American society."

In 1826, Masonry in America suffered an enormous set-back. One of the good citizens of America, William Morgan, disappeared after threatening to publish the Masonic secrets. The Masons, on supposition, got the blame. Anti-Masonic feeling abounded and Masonry was virtually driven underground. It was not until the 1850's that the revival had taken place.

During this period, the "Anti-Masonic Party" was formed. Its organisers made use of the wave of anti-Masonic feeling to form a new political party to oppose the rising Jacksonian democracy. It was only in 1831, when they put forward William Wirt as their choice for the Presidency that they holed their cause below the water-line. Wirt was not only a Freemason but defended the Order before the very convention that nominated him. Freemasons obviously have their uses, even to anti-Masonic organisations.

Before the turn of the century, Americans were somewhat Victorian in their approach to propriety. Masonically, saloon-keepers were frowned upon. In 1895 the Grand Lodge of Texas held an appraisal of its membership. Of the 26,000 members it was found that over 400 "drank to excess"! Just how they came by such information, or how accurate it was, is not evident, but its refreshing to know that the present day topers in the ranks of the Masons are not without precedent.

Without a doubt Freemasonry flourished throughout early America. By 1880 there were 9000 lodges. To put this figure into prospective it must be realised that approximately 8500 lodges come under the auspices of the Grand Lodge of England at the present time.

During the 1800's, the simplistic Masonic attitude to prayer brought the early American Masons into a scenario of conflict with the bitter sectarianism which raged between the various religious denominations. Methodist, Presbyterian and Baptist ministers would take care to avoid one another, whilst Masonry provided a unifying bond for its participants. As such religions have a basic, common aim, one could be forgiven for pondering as to whether religious arguments are actually about religion, or the proportion of cash resulting in the individual collection boxes.

Americans do things in grand style, not least the American Masons. When they erected the Masonic Temple in Chicago in 1894, it boasted twenty-two stories and was the highest building in the world. The Oakland Temple is particularly opulent, numerous American dollars having funded its building, decoration and furnishings. These, and other Masonic edifices, led to the castigation of the American Masons by their contempories for "immortalising themselves, and their history, in bricks and mortar."

This is a churlish premise. No one would argue that Masons, not only in America, but the rest of the world as well, have put up some pretty impressive stuff. But let us not lose sight of the fact that the erection of impressive structures is not only confined to speculative Masons. The erection of any monumental edifice is not only lasting testimony to those who provide the cash, it is a lasting tribute, for better or for worse, to the man who designed it. There is nothing an architect likes better than to be given a commission with no financial restrictions! This usually represents a once-in-a-lifetime opportunity to commend himself to posterity.

In line with most other forms of construction, modern Masonic building takes thermal efficiency into consideration before aesthetics. Cost effectiveness is now a prime consideration in all such matters. The pyramids and the Taj Mahal would never have risen towards the sky had they been under the scrutiny of a diligent quantity surveyor banging away with a calculator.

Controversy has permeated other aspects of American Freemasonry throughout the years. In the 1920's, The Grand Master of Oregon found it necessary to address the question of the Ku Klux Klan within the ranks of his members.

Far be it from any Englishman to get involved with that particular argument, but the existence of the Prince Hall school of thought most definitely *is* questioned by the higher echelons in England.

It was the actual formation of the Prince Hall Grand Lodges that upsets Her Majesty's Masonic subjects. The constitution was set up independently and did not observe the procedures as practised. Seemingly, everything else in that organisation conformed to the precepts - but the tolerance of Masonry in general does not allow for the formation of lodges without permission and supervision from on high. Some American Masons recognise Prince Hall, some do not. Even within the ranks of Masons differences do exist, but it is desirable that such differences are dealt with peaceably and not in an atmosphere of mayhem.

England has the Grand Order of Lady Masons, America has the Eastern Star. The Eastern Star are the Lady Masons of America. Again, there is no actual connection between male and female, with the difference that, at certain meetings of the Eastern Star, it is necessary for a male Mason to be present.

I actually knew a male English Mason who used to attend meetings of the Eastern Star when in America. I can now impart this knowledge without evasion, equivocation or mental reservation of any kind as, unfortunately, our Brother has departed this mortal toil and is at peace in the Grand Lodge Above - I hope! Were he still amongst us there would be those in England who, given this information, would be unrolling a carpet, from which stand-point, he would be suitably admonished. The attendance, by an English Mason, of lodges which are not officially recognised by Grand Lodge of England is simply not allowed.

American Masonry boasts an aspect of which we in Britain have no equivalent; The Shriners! These gentlemen represent Uncle Sam's brethren in their most colourful and demonstrative form.

In order to join this select band, one must have taken thirty or more degrees but, this done, one is permitted to engage oneself in the activities of a club within a club. They have their own very colourful uniform and are to be seen indulging themselves in the social activities of America, such are described at the beginning of this chapter.

Americans have a shorter history than many countries in the world, and their demonstrativeness is often symbolised by fierce patriotism - not least the American Masons. At the start of the First World War, the Stars and Stripes was introduced into every lodge-room in America.

It is very difficult to play the numbers game with America. In Britain, the average lodge consists of between fifty and seventy members. In America, lodges number their members in hundreds. A simple statistic which will boggle the minds those British Masons, not already privy to the information, is that the Palestine Lodge in Detroit has some 4000 members - personally, I was left wondering what would happen if they all turned up on the same night.

It did come to my notice that the question is asked why, because of the size of American lodges statistically, some secretaries and treasurers remain in office over-long and hog the positions. Even allowing for the numbers in the membership, this is probably a somewhat arbitrary point. If it is anything like England, the secretaries and treasurers remain in office throughout the years quite simply because nobody else wants the job.

It must be something to do with the
American constitution.

I know one member who is the secretary of three lodges. From my own humble stand-point I can only feel that the poor fellow must suffer from nightmares.

Before ending this chapter, one point will no doubt be of interest to Masons on both sides of the Atlantic - and the rest of the world. Differences in the practice of Masonry in England and America are not all that great bearing in mind that circumstances and physical distance have separated our constitutions.

I have already observed that Bristol is peculiar to itself. But, to experience far greater differences in Masonic practices, the English Mason would not have to travel the 3000 odd miles to America. He would merely travel North across that piece of masonry, and I now mean bricks and mortar, that Hadrian erected to defend our country. The Scots have traditions which differ in many ways from those the Englishman has come to regard as standard. I have not experienced these first hand, but am given to believe that the trip would be well worthwhile.

No doubt there are many British Masons who would enjoy visiting one of those lodges under the fifty-one Grand Lodges in the distant West. In saying this, it is worthy of mention that, if a British Mason were to visit America, or vice versa - or for that matter, any Mason of any country visit any other lodge of any other country in the world, he would not be known as coming from his country of origin. The distance he had travelled would doubtless add an extra fascination to his presence but, in whatever lodge he found himself, he would simply be known as "Brother."

The hands do stretch across the sea and it may be considered worthy of note that those hands are extended in friendship, and in the true spirit of Freemasonry as it is dictated that it ought to be practised.

No, We're Not a Funny Bunch of People!

Chapter: Eleven.

I Didn't Know He Was One of Those.

The title of this chapter augurs an air of unacceptability towards the subject under scrutiny, but so often such a remark is made by members of the outside world when the knowledge is imparted that someone is a member of the Masonic Fraternity. Announcement of involvement is greeted with a quizzical or bemused air which suggests the receiver of such news must be, in some way, apprehensive.

Having got this far, it may be sincerely hoped that non Masonic readers will have, by now, begun to realise that there is absolutely nothing to be apprehensive about. Quizzical and bemused - Yes! I sincerely trust that I have managed to stir the imaginations of those who have joined me on this journey. I trust a clearer picture has formed itself in the minds of the previously apprehensive and I modestly hope that I have done something to further a very deserving cause.

There are those persons, far greater in status and stature than I, who have been proud to be associated with the Masonic movement and I trust that History will show that the future will see Freemasonry enjoying the membership of many more similarly illustrious people. Having said this, let us not detract from the standing of the foot-soldiers of Masonry. Without the ordinary, there cannot be the sublime and without a base, an apex has no foundation.

King Edward VII was the most illustrious Mason to grace the English scene. Not only was his social status supreme, his Masonic standing could not have been higher. He was Grand Master from 1874 until 1901.

On the other side of the Atlantic, the first American President, George Washington was a very keen Mason. Military involvement in Masonry is well known and Washington enjoyed great solace in the knowledge that many of his officers were fellow Masons. Washington was the first of many American Presidents to join the ranks of the Brethren. Theodore Roosevelt's involvement was apparent in my chapter on our colonial cousins but his namesake, Franklin also figured, along with Benjamin Franklin, Harry Truman and Gerald Ford. Harry Truman actually rose to become Grand Master of Missouri.

The military interest in America has continued through the passage of time with many of America's top service names counting themselves among our members, not least General Douglas MacArthur.

In the dark days of the 1940's, the greatest military force ever assembled came together under the leadership of a Mason who subsequently joined the illustrious ranks of those privileged to have held the office of President of the United States of America. The whole world was embroiled in conflict because of the ambitions of a certain Austrian painter and decorator; when the time for retribution approached, the Supreme Commander of the Allied forces was Brother Ike.

General Eisenhower had an equally illustrious colleague on the Eastern shore of the Atlantic. Thus said, Brother Churchill may have had an illustrious career politically but, sad to say, his Masonic career was not one that will go down in with distinction in the annals of

Masonry. Winston Spencer Churchill joined Freemasonry, but subsequently resigned, as a Master Mason, after only eleven years of membership. No one knows precisely why he resigned, but Winnie was Masonry's loss. The paradoxical facts of this matter are that our revered Prime Minister was a keen operative Mason - he loved laying bricks. His famous wall in the county of Kent has featured in numerous stories surrounding Winston. He regarded its construction as, not only interesting, but therapeutic. And, whereas Ike was a great golfing enthusiast, Brother Churchill was less enamoured by the prospects. He is on record as saying that, "Golf a is good walk, spoiled!"

It was from America that we had the many tales of "How the West was won." From these stories came the cowboy films. In the early versions there was always a happy ending - no matter what had gone on previously - "Those pesky injuns have shot ma wife, killed ma cattle and burned down ma ranch. Now a'm gonna get those pesky injuns - but jus' before ar do, ar's gonna sing you a little song!"

Brother Cecil B. DeMille may or may not have been operating the cameras, and our Brethren may or may not have been vocalists, but Brothers Tom Mix, Gene Autrey, Kit Carson and Buffalo Bill Cody certainly rode out into the sunset. Probably the most famous cowboy of all will be remembered, not only for his screen roles, but for his last courageous fight. After a stalwart battle he lost that fight, but Brother John Wayne will ever be remembered for the courage he showed during that last period of his existence, as well as for the many pleasurable hours of entertainment which he gave mankind.

The good citizens of Southport in Lancashire, England, have erected a plaque in honour of an American Mason. They placed it in the middle of a conglomeration of bushes. To the uninformed, this display of affection may appear somewhat bizarre - until it is explained that the actual location of the plaque is near to the Fifteenth hole on the Royal Birkdale Golf Course. It was in the 1950's that a young American golfer first began to make his mark on the international scene. He became the first of the great charismatic golfers. He drew vast crowds wherever he played, crowds which were known as "Arnie's Army" - crowds which made our subject the first "Pop-Star" of golf.

In 1961 he was leading the British Open from the Welshman, Dai Rees, when helped by high winds, he drove his tee-shot into the aforementioned bushes. The ball came to rest in an impossible lie, choked by a mixture of grass and scrub.

There was a carry of some 140 yards between the golfer and the green, leaving a prospect which was hardly for the faint hearted. It is worthy of mention that this intrepid sportsman was later to advocate conservatism when in such trouble but, on this occasion, he manfully wielded a six-iron and, with a crashing blow, deposited the ball on the green. He went on to win the Open.

Such a shot could only happen in the wildest dreams of the average exponent of the game of the Royal and Ancients. It was a shot worthy of recognition, and recognised it was. The plaque commemorates the ability, and the shot, of Brother Arnold Palmer.

There is a Masonic banner on the Moon! This snippet of information was hushed up for a long time - not by the Masons, but by the American establishment. The Brother who surreptitiously placed this piece of heraldry

I wish they'd send Buzz Aldrin up with a new
banner. This one's getting a bit tatty after all
this time.

in situ was Buzz Aldrin during the Apollo 11 flight. The reasons for annoyance have not been officially tabulated. It is, therefore, open to conjecture as to whether the wrath was generated by mere chain-of-command or possible political motives.

My old friend Ben, on hearing this story, was heard to say, "Do you know how much fuel it would have taken to get that thing up there?"

Conservation of fuel was always high on the list of Ben's professional priorities. He is an ex-airline pilot.

Transport was an over-riding concern in another famous American Brother's mind. "They can have a car in any colour so long as it's black" said Henry Ford.

Apart from heading his empire, this worthy Mason was also Master of the Palestine Lodge in Detroit.

Harmony is sought by the exponents of Masonry and harmony is also sought by the musical Masons; Count Basie, Duke Ellington, W.C. Handy, Paul Robeson and Nat King Cole would have been happy to oblige. Masonry can also lay claim to the inclusion of the originators of musical harmony amongst its members. Mozart, Sibelius, Phillip John Souza, Irving Berlin and Sir Arthur Sullivan were all Masons.

Not only was the institution fortunate to have one of Britain's most famous composers as a member, the Grand Lodge of England was also privileged to have Sir Arthur Sullivan as its organist. With his partner and fellow Mason, Sir William Gilbert, Sullivan endowed the British nation, and for that matter, the rest of the world with a priceless legacy.

Harmony in life was also sought, but not ideally achieved, by another Mason, Brother Martin Luther King.

The professional harmony of Jack Dempsey, Jack Johnson and Sugar Ray Robinson would seem to defeat the object of the exercise but, having concluded their pugilistics, they were found to be included in our ranks.

The entertainment world not only necessitates the talents of entertainers and sportsmen, it requires the provision of entertainment venues. It was from Canada that a young entrepreneur set forth for the shores of England. He was far sighted and a great visionary in his own right. He established a whole new scenario in Britain and became known as the "Father of the Holiday Camps." His intuitive genius provided the British people with a holiday which was not at the mercy of Britain's somewhat inclement weather and through him, millions of people have had the opportunity of a good holiday without having to travel abroad.

The young man who left Canada not only benefited himself and his clients. In latter years he not only gave away many thousands of pounds to charity, he spent many hours working on behalf of charity. He is, unfortunately, no longer with us; but his memory lingers on. I do not suppose the reader will be too surprised when I say that Sir Billy Butlin was a Mason.

In writing on the subject of Freemasonry I follow in distinguished footsteps. Brother Rudyard Kipling and Brother Robbie Burns both waxed forth loquacious on the subject - although the Scots are still in the process of preparing a translation so that the English Masons might understand what our kilted Brother was on about.

Through writers such as these, the story of Masonry has spread, yet to say it spread merely by the written word would be inaccurate as many of the great explorers, travellers and statesmen were Freemasons, not least, Sir

Walter Scott, Scott of the Antarctic, Lord Kitchener, Charles Lindberg and Garibaldi - who for a time was the Grand Master of Palermo.

All these distinguished people have played a part in our history; a history of which they are proud, and a history which is proud of them. The members I have mentioned are but a few. There are many more whose names could fill these pages if circumstances permitted, but practicality prevents such a exercise.

I will end this part of my work by mentioning just one more distinguished Mason. His name is Harold Green. There will be those among the readership to whom this name will not be familiar, and the reason for his inclusion in this particular chapter will not be immediately clear.

Harold Green is a member of Addey and Stanhope Lodge which meets at Freemasons Hall in London. He has been a member of that lodge since 1936, and for the first fifty-five years of his membership did not miss a single meeting. He has since missed just one! - through ill health. Without people such as Harold the foundations of Masonry would crumble. They are the backbone of our institution and an inspiration to us all. The Grand Lodge of England has officially recognised this Brother's devotion and loyalty, and added its gratitude by way of correspondence.

We have had, and still do have, many famous and noteworthy members in our ranks. I am sure that they, and all the distinguished Masons I have mentioned, would join with me in adding our congratulations and finishing this chapter with the good name of Brother Harold.

No, We're Not a Funny Bunch of People!

Chapter: Twelve.

Receive with Grace and Give with Gratitude.

There cannot be a Mason in this world who, at some stage in his life, has not had sufficient funds to gratify his immediate requirements and who will not remember his feelings at that particular moment.

This kind of experience will not be peculiar to Masons. There are many people who in their life have found themselves in financial extremities, whether immediate, or of a more lasting nature. There will be few motorists who will not be familiar with the situation of having filled the tank, finding themselves in the wrong pair of trousers, thus having no money or credit cards to honour their financial obligations.

Having become a member of the Masonic Movement, a Mason begins to receive its several benefits. These are not material benefits but benefits which immediately entitle him to participate in an institution which is world-wide.

Having merely taken his First Degree, the newly admitted Mason is quite at liberty to take a trip on Concorde, the first lady pilot of which I am privileged to know personally, and attend a First Degree meeting in the Land of the Free - or anywhere in the world for that matter. There are not too many organisations which give their members this kind of latitude. This is not a bad return for having received membership, thus such membership should surely be received with grace, and then the opportunity to give, be embraced with gratitude.

The Waters of Salvation are Free - thus sayeth the old adage. The Waters of Salvation may well be free, but it is a practical fact of life that someone has to pay for the pump.

It is incumbent on every Mason on the face of this Earth to divvy up in the cause of Charity. This is the overriding factor in all Masonic circles and Charity's cause is met by all the Brethren throughout the world. Not only is it met - it is met with cheerfulness and a genuine desire to help those whose need is apparent and deserving. In meeting this requirement, the Masons do not solicit assistance from outside sources. They raise the money entirely from within the confines of their own ranks.

The only possible exception to this is at social functions. Non Masonic guests are permitted at all functions, during the course of which there may well be a raffle in the cause of charity. Various garden parties and fêtes are also arranged, the prime object of which is the raising of charitable funds. Again, in such instances, non Masonic guests are not only permitted, but are welcomed.

A point worthy of clarification now comes to mind as being worthy of mention. Within the parlance of Masonry, reference is frequently made to our "Masonic Charities." There are two kinds of Masonic Charities - those Charities which are directly administered by the Masonic bodies themselves, and those Charities to which the Masonic world donates funds, but is not subsequently involved in the channelling of those funds. Both come under the heading of "Masonic Charities."

In England and Wales the main Charities which come under the Masonic umbrella are the Grand Charity, which is the governing body overseeing all charitable donations; The New Samaritan Fund which takes care of all those needing hospital treatment; The Royal Masonic Benevolent Institute, the branch which looks after widows and the sick; and The Masonic Trust for Girls and Boys, the main object of this branch being the provision for orphans, covering educational requirements as well as other needs.

We did have a hospital - indeed we do still have a hospital, but, as though to provide a perfect example of how disagreement can filter into the structure of Masonry, it will doubtless be recalled by some readers how, in 1992, the Royal Masonic Hospital became the subject of some quite substantial press coverage.

The basic problem centred round a disagreement as to how the hospital should be run. The dispute was not about medicine, it was basically about the allocation of funds.

As is democratically necessary, the dispute was referred to the membership - and I mean the whole membership. This made the dispute cumbersome. The subject was debated in every lodge in the Country.

As was their wont, the Brethren listened attentively to what was being said but, as the Hospital is situated in London, total comprehension did not come easily to the Brethren ensconced in the far distant parts of the Realm.

After much discussion over internal problems, the Duke of Kent and Prince Michael of Kent resigned from their positions on the Hospital authority. This caused the Board of General Purposes to withdraw its support for the Hospital and common dissent was, unfortunately, apparent.

This kind of dispute takes place every day in commercial practice - and at the end of the day, a Hospital not coming under the Health Service has to be run on commercial grounds. But because the subject concerned the Masons, and their Royal Hignesses were involved, the media attention was that much more intense.

The Hospital is now run by its own Board. A simple solution one would have thought. Not only that, it is running efficiently and effectively. The dust has settled and, once again, the various ailments of Man can be cured under the roof of the Royal Masonic Hospital, albeit scrutinised by accountants.

Accountants have a wonderful way of knowing what *ought* to be happening. They draw graphs to this effect and one wonders if the accountants at the Hospital do actually appreciate those graphs produced by their medical colleagues which depict that which is *actually* occurring to their patients. It can be assumed, with no small degree of confidence, that Nature has not yet taken her degree in financial accountancy. Accountancy, Yes! - but financial accountancy, No!

Although other charities are supported, the greater proportion of Charities supported by the Grand Lodge of England and Wales concern themselves with the sick and the children. This is likewise true of the extra mural Charities supported outside the immediate Masonic movement.

In 1992, some £300,000 was given by our Grand Lodge to outside Charities - the full list of which is available for inspection at Freemason's Hall. The entire, enormously wide-ranging list of close to three hundred worthy causes, includes, for example, the Greater London Association for Disabled People and the Surrey Docks Play Association, the Burma Star Association is there, likewise the London Taxi Drivers Fund for Underprivileged Children. The Association of Teachers of Lip-reading Adults features alongside the Cot death

Society and, geographically diverse, the Bath Institute for Rheumatic Diseases is included with the Sheffield Children's Hospital.

These are but a few of the worthy causes supported by the Masons of England and Wales through the channels of our Grand Lodge.

Beside the Charities which are actually listed several unsung donations are made. Until recently, it was the practice of the British Masons to donate an entire Life-Boat to the Service when circumstances permitted. Even now, in times of more specialised craft, it is the custom to furnish the institution with such equipment as may be deemed necessary.

Charity is also supported by lodges on a local basis. If there is a local charity which is attached to a lodge, or the incumbent master for the year is desirous of assisting a cause of his choice, then support will be forthcoming from local Brethren. This form of local support is a direct contribution. It does not show up on the figures supplied by Grand Lodge.

The aged, the sick, the infirm, the needy, are all supported without trappings or fuss. The contributions which make these provisions possible are willingly given by all the Brethren throughout, not only England and Wales, but the rest of the world. At every single Masonic meeting there is a collection in aid of Charity, in addition to which the members make an annual, lump sum contribution. A proportion of every members yearly subscription also goes to Charity.

The Charities which are close to home are, obviously, the ones with which I am most familiar, but it is now apposite that I take the reader back to the land of

I'm afraid you'll have to go to the Grand Lodge Below. When the Provincial Grand Master asked you for a contribution to the building fund, you shouldn't have sent him an old bag of rock hard cement!

numbers, where the sheer weight of influence allows things to occur, which do not occur anywhere else on this Earth.

It almost goes without saying that what has been described as the "greatest Masonic charitable institution in the world" is to be found in America. The Elizabethtown Homes in Pennsylvania stand in over 1,000 acres comprising more than twenty buildings in cultivated areas allotted to farming, gardening and orchards. The establishment can accommodate up to one-thousand people, yet this great charity boasts one facet which is peculiar to itself. The whole establishment is run on a totally confidential basis. Nothing is publicised as to how those afforded its benefits arrive or depart. The Charity is given with complete privacy to the receiver and no public recognition is sought by the establishment.

Let us conclude my observations on Charity by giving Uncle Sam's Masonic Brethren due recognition. My British counterparts pay their corner, and as I have already premised, they do it willingly. Thus acknowledged, I am sure they will not object to my letting our American Brothers have the glory at the end of this chapter of benefactors.

In 1992, our Brethren across the water gave a staggering $400,000,000 to Charity.

A good compere knows when to come off - and after a statement like that, there is nothing left to say - except possibly, on behalf of Masons everywhere, to add our congratulations.

Well done chaps! I will fill my glass with my usual mixture of potencies and drink to your health at the first available opportunity!

No, We're Not a Funny Bunch of People!

Chapter: Thirteen

The Long and the Short of It.

"How old is mother?"

To the unenlightened, a strange and seemingly impertinent question. To the everyday Mason the information requested is simple and pragmatic.

The question is not pertinent to the age of man's maternal progenitor. The person is merely enquiring as to the number and thus the relative age of the Mason's Mother Lodge.

Antiquity has its own inherent way of breeding snobbery, consequently, whereas the snobbery is underlying in Masonry, it cannot be concealed that it is, in fact, there.

There is a degree of kudos to be derived from the knowledge that one was initiated into an old established lodge. Before my initiation, I remember the observation: "You do, of course, realise that you will be joining a lodge which is over One-Hundred years old!"

A certain amount of reflected glory is to be achieved by becoming a joining member of such an establishment, having been initiated in another quarter, but there is a definite satisfaction attained when a Masons career begins amidst the paraphernalia of a lodge which can boast a long and distinguished history.

If, at the Festive Board, a toast is drunk to the "Founders of the Lodge" and no-one stands up to receive the toast due to the simple fact they have all gone to the Grand Lodge Above, Below or in Between, depending on their conduct in life, then one may rightly assume that one is in the company of those Masons whose predecessors in that lodge must have been many in number. If, when such a toast is drunk, the founders stand up like trees in the forest, the span of existence of that lodge will not be all that great.

The oldest lodge in England is Lodge of Antiquity No.2. This flagship of English Masonry meets in London, its position not being pre-empted by a Lodge No.1. Lodge No.1, in England, was formed after Lodge No.2.

In earlier days, the lodge numbers were shuffled as lodges were formed or disbanded. Thus the numbers of the early lodges do not necessarily correspond to their chronological existence. All lodges in modern times have been formed in numerical order. Should a lodge cease to exist, its number becomes defunct.

The Province of Sussex is home to "the oldest lodge in Sussex" and "the oldest Sussex lodge."

The oldest lodge in Sussex is the Howard Lodge of Brotherly Love No.56, the oldest Sussex lodge being the Lodge of Union No.38. My observation of the shuffling of numbers is again exemplified. The Lodge of Union was formed in 1812 by the union of two other lodges, but the Great Grandmother of Sussex remains the Howard Lodge which was first formed in 1736.

The specific reason for the slight variation in titles is that the Howard Lodge originated in London, transferring to Sussex in 1789.

In one of the earlier chapters, I made reference to secretaries and art forms. The Secretary of the Howard Lodge was just such a one as I had in mind. John's performance in this position approaches theatrical levels and is highly entertaining. One of the traditions of the Lodge is that an old minute, from days gone by, is read at every meeting. This is duly done. Fortunately, it has been my privilege to be provided with a selection of these minutes. Having perused them, it was immediately obvious that the Masonic topers had struck again! I reproduce one of the minutes from the meeting of 14th June, 1802.

"The Master proposed that the motion made last Lodge meeting night respecting Bro. Jonathon R......'s being raised to the Third Degree be rescinded on account of his attending the Lodge in a state of intoxication, which being duly seconded, was ordered accordingly."

It will be, I trust, remembered that I made the observation that harmony is always sought. We have to acknowledge, however, that that which we seek is not always attained. This is obvious from a minute of the 5th June, 1801:

"Bro. Gregson proposed that Bro. F...... be severely reprimanded by the Master in open Lodge in consequence of very improper language made use of by said Bro. F......, which being duly seconded, was ordered accordingly; it was also agreed that if he does not appear after receiving a regular summons for that purpose, the said Bro. F...... be expelled from the Lodge in due form."

It was not only the mere lay brethren who came under fire. The minutes of the meeting on 20th March, 1890 had this inclusion:

"W.Bro. Francis moved that the Lodge views with great regret and dissatisfaction the manner in which the Secretary discharges the duties of his office both with regard to finances and keeping the records and returns of the Lodge and humbly begs to call the master's attention to a state of things which cannot but be highly prejudicial to the interests of the Lodge. Bro. Neame seconded the motion. The acting Master put the motion to the Lodge. The motion was carried unanimously."

Despite all the aspirations and ideals which are laid down for our guidance, it seems the good brethren still appear to have a pop at one another from time to time. Happily, sympathy is evinced on other occasions. Viz the minutes on 15th October, 1802:

"The acting Master proposed that the money paid by Mr. Chas. R...... of Burham for his proposition fee be returned on account of his mental derangement, which was ordered accordingly."

This minute will, no doubt, give great satisfaction to those who, through the passage of time, have been convinced that all Masons, or prospective Masons, have lost their marbles.

An air of indifference seems to have manifested itself on one particular occasion. Bro. De'ath was the subject of a minute of the meeting of the 18th May, 1900:

"Bro. De'ath having answered the necessary questions retired from the Lodge. The Lodge was opened in the Third Degree."

At this juncture Bro. De'ath must have decided that time was of the essence and would not permit his intended course. He therefore changed his schedule. The minute continued -

"Bro. De'ath having notified to the Master that he was obliged to leave to catch his train, his being raised to the Third Degree was postponed to the next meeting."

Earlier in this work, I made the observation that lodges do not, in fact, go on through the night. This observation is evinced in a minute of the meeting dated 8th October, 1797:

"Resolved that the Lodge be closed on each night before 11 o'clock under a penalty of Two-shillings and six-pence to be paid by the Master."

At that time the Lodge and the Festive Board were one and overlapped. Shut down was somewhat later than it is now, but the whole set-up was far more parochial, the problems of distance and transport not being so prevalent.

These historical minutes are not only amusing, they give a wonderful insight of past proceedings to those brethren whose lodges were founded in the Twentieth Century. Let us come up to date. A minute from the meeting on 19th February, 1987 ran thus:

"On a report Bro. Inner Guard announced the presence of the police without, making enquiries as to the ownership of a white Cavalier car which had left the car park and come to rest in the road outside the Temple. After a period indicating mature consideration, a well known Bro. of Sincerity Lodge departed to retrieve the situation - and his car."

It is interesting to note that John records the present day minutes in a style which is faithful to that of his predecessors. The humorous element is retained, yet it reflects the traditions of a lodge which, not so long ago, celebrated its two and a half centuries of existence.

The Grand Lodge of England and Wales enjoyed its Two-Hundred and Seventy-Fifth Anniversary in 1992. It was a celebrated occasion and was held at Earls Court. For the first time in history, the Grand Lodge was viewed by millions on the Haunted Fish Tank. Television cameras allowed the public their first glimpse of what actually takes place.

The "Powers that Be" were pleased with the reception which they received and the occasion was enjoyed by all who had the opportunity to participate. It is, however, worthy of emphasis that that landmark was only the

Naturally Carruthers, as I am assured you won't
be driving home, it will be my pleasure to buy
you one for the road.

anniversary of unification. Masonry had been practised in individual groups long before the various factions united and came together under one banner.

Freemasonry has been in existence for a very long time. Furthermore, it may be noted with pride, that it has endured, and overcome, some fairly arduous set backs. The journey through time has been fraught with, not only the unhappy circumstances which surround mankind in general, but has been accompanied by the unnecessary and undeserved prejudices. In less enlightened times, Masons were actually tortured for their beliefs, although this kind of practice was not only restricted, historically, to Masons.

During times of conflict, Masonic prisoners-of-war carried on their craft by making the necessary accoutrements from waste material in the prison camps. Examples of these are displayed in the Museum and Library at Freemasons Hall in London. A fact which will not be widely known, or appreciated, is that this Museum and Library are open to the general public.

The dissolution of the Communist world discovered the continued existence of Masonry in countries such as Poland and Czechoslovakia. At the time of writing it is speculative as to whether the Freemasons of Russia may or may not have survived.

The prejudice against Masonry has made its presence felt in several different forms. The Press have had their periodic broadsides aimed at us.

The producers of television have seen fit to show ill-advised - and I mean "ill-advised" in its very literal sense - documentaries which were so obviously one-sided as to be highly questionable.

Thus said, they could possibly be forgiven for this as it is only very recently that anyone from within our ranks has been prepared to meet any prejudice head-on. Information from the hierarchy has not always been available or forthcoming.

In recent years we have been the subject of three particular investigative books.

The first of these was "Darkness Visible" which was written by the Reverend Walton Hannah. This enterprising cleric, although not a Mason, actually gained admission to a Masonic lodge and commemorated the occasion by committing his experiences to print.

Masonically, one should be seen to be aligned with the wringing of hands, gnashing of teeth and sack-cloth and ashes syndrome that followed this embarrassment to our Masonic fortunes. Privately however, one cannot help but admire the fellow's ingenuity. I would be leading the reader astray if I did not record that I do not know how he achieved entry. Furthermore, were anyone to repeat the exercise, I have no idea, were they not a Mason, how they would manage it.

It is the duty of the Junior Warden to ensure that all present are duly qualified. Someone boobed somewhere. It is a sobering thought that someone, somewhere, must be going round with the title of "Provincial Grand Jackass" in consequence of our unexpected visitor.

The foundations of Masonry suffered the proverbial earth tremor.

The second book written in 1984 by Stephen Knight was entitled "The Brotherhood." It was a well written, entertaining book and was a best seller. Unfortunately, as far as Masonry was concerned, it was inaccurate and written with an obvious bias against Masonry.

Again, the foundations were the subject of a tremor - and mumblings went on within the body of the institution. There was no malice. Indignation - bemusement - hurt - questions as to why we were continuously the subject of scrutiny - but the shoulders were shrugged, and life went on.

Life went on for Masonry but, regrettably, it was not so for the author. He was to suffer a tragic end after a long illness.

Stephen Knight had written about Masons and Masonry, but there is not a genuine Mason on this Earth who would have wished to see Stephen Knight's demise, much less the sad ending that befell him. He had a tilt at Masonry - Yes! But Masons are not bitter people. Not only Stephen Knight, but anyone in extremities, would be helped if it were at all possible.

It is quoted within its own writings that "Masonry has survived the wreck of mighty empires and the destroying hand of time." This is true - and it did not happen because its members were all a bunch of villains. Remember the famous names in one of the former chapters and ask the question - "Why?!" - Why, if some of the stories are to be believed, do these famous and distinguished people bother to associate themselves with a bunch of thieves, vagabonds and layabouts.

Consider just one, His Majesty, King Edward VII. He had nothing to gain socially, he had nothing to gain Masonically - so "Why?!"

There can be no tangible answer - if the voices of disdain are to be believed. It therefore necessarily follows that the members of Masonry join together, in the spirit of Brotherhood, with the aim of social enjoyment for themselves and a desire to benefit the world in general.

The story was long, but the writer was Short! The writer of the third book on Freemasonry, "Inside the Brotherhood" was an author by the name of Martin Short. It was with the publication of this book in 1989 that the Masonic patience and sense of humour were tried to the limit.

This book was written with an acrimonious attitude that the Masons found odious. It was a volume which was based on hypotheses and wild speculation, and is the work to which I have been largely referring throughout this book.

What Martin Short actually did was to get his hands on Stephen Knight's notes and attempt to jump on a band wagon. He spent four years in research and writing the book, four years in which he did his very best to destroy the credibility of Freemasonry.

The powers that be were aware that he was writing a book on Masonry, thus Mr. Short was asked if there were any way in which they could be of assistance as they were desirous that any publication should give two sides of any story or situation.

Friend Short ignored all such approaches. This was simply because he had no intention of putting down anything which might be considered complimentary.

He, therefore, spent four years plotting destruction. Hardly an exercise in self satisfaction. It therefore follows that Martin Short can have nothing to gain personally - except cash! - and when the motive is purely financial the credence of the perpetrator must be directly proportional to the number of pieces of silver involved.

Even for this the Masons would still probably forgive Mr. Short. He is an author and a journalist, and as such, it befits his situation that he turns his attention to some subject or other on which to write. He can be forgiven for the motive of profit. It is necessary for every mortal on this planet to procure a crust from somewhere. He can even be forgiven for his acrimonious and belligerent attitude. The Masons have taken the flak before, and no doubt will be called on to do so again. He can be forgiven for most of his hypothesis and speculation - something has to fill the pages between the covers of any book.

There is one observation however, for which, even with the greatest degree of charity in mind, Mr. Short cannot be forgiven. By this I mean the hypothesis which concerns the demise of Stephen Knight.

By a highly speculative theory, more in keeping with the confines of Darth Vador and Star Wars than a serious literary exercise, Martin Short puts forward a supposition which suggests that, because of what he had written about them, the Masons were instrumental in Stephen Knight's end. It was an insinuation which was unkind, unjustified, and smacked of malice in the extreme.

The passage of time has, thankfully, nullified Mr. Short's theory. Had his premise been correct and someone or something with the title of "Grand Exterminator" been in existence, used for dispatching dissenters against Masonry, it necessarily follows that friend Short would also have been duly dispatched to pastures new.

This exercise would probably have been somewhat expedient as there was not the sneaking regard for Mr. Short which his preceding authors enjoyed.

Martin Short is still walking the face of this Earth today so his theory is without foundation. Most of the things in his book were without foundation. Only occasionally did he put his head above the parapet and put down something as categorical fact - and then he got it wrong! I will give just one example.

At one stage in his book he describes the First Degree sign in Freemasonry as "drawing the first finger of the hand across the throat implying 'to cut'." What friend Short was describing is, in fact, the international sign for "cut." However, I would assure Mr. Short, and everyone else reading this book, that it is most definitely not the First Degree sign in Freemasonry. How much credence can be given to the rest of his work I leave to each individual mind.

It is a fact of life that tolerance levels are tried in extremities. It is to their very great credit that the Masons have maintained their tolerance levels throughout their trials and tribulations. This cannot be said of Mr. Short. Towards the end of his book he unkindly suggests that the names and addresses of Masons should be posted in places such as libraries so that the world may know who these purported charlatans are.

I notice that his address is not made available lest I should wish to get my copy autographed, or the former members of P.2. Lodge from Italy wish to congratulate him on their inclusion in his pernicious volume.

Despite all its critics and set backs, Freemasonry abounds today. Not only does it abound, it does so in a spirit of good natured humour which belies those who would seek to discredit it. Let us, therefore, finish this chapter in good humour by returning to the Minute Book of the Howard Lodge of Brotherly Love. It was at the meeting of 7th December, 1799 that the principles and tenets got fractionally mixed up. A minute from the meeting ran thus:

"Charles L...... was regularly proposed and balloted for in the usual manner and rejected by 5 black balls."

"All business being over, the Lodge was closed in due form with harmony and brotherly love."

Not everything in our system is perfect. The system does, sometimes, go wrong - but when it does, we are the first to admit it!

No, We're Not a Funny Bunch of People!

Chapter: Fourteen.

This Toast must be the Last.

It is with a degree of sadness that I approach the end of this book, the greater part of which was written in 1992, thus, another year has come and another has gone since its inception.

In that year a great deal occurred. The Great Architect, fortuitously for me, allowed me the pleasure of celebrating the tenth anniversary of my fortieth birthday. I got my Provincial Gong from the Provincial Grand Master of Sussex - one only hopes that my endeavours contain nothing which will prompt him to ask for it back.

1992 was the year in which I finally settled down to write something that I had wanted to write for years and I hope that, somehow, I have been able to present my subject from a central stand-point, or at least from a stand-point from which conclusions can be reached which are not necessarily prejudicial.

Not everyone or everything in this life, or on this Earth are always what they first appear. Thus it is sometimes desirable to stand back and reflect on the attributes and drawbacks of people, circumstances and institutions before a hardening of opinion sets in. Let us not forget that Al Capone's business card described him as a "Second Hand Furniture Salesman" and that Charlie Chaplin entered a "Charlie Chaplin Look-alike" competition in Monte Carlo - and came third!

To fully understand anything or any subject, it goes without saying that experience is necessary. Any writer can expound prolifically on any subject, going into great and minute detail, but his readers are still without the benefit of practical experience. Even anticipation of experience is not always accurate - consider that submariners do not suffer from sea sickness. They suffer from a form of air-sickness.

To be fully understood, therefore, Masonry must be experienced. What I have tried to do is to clarify certain issues relating to Masonry, and sincerely trust that a proportion of readers will have found the subject interesting enough to seek to join our numbers.

I have observed during this work that the dictates as laid down should enhance the moral standing of all men within our ranks. I have also acknowledged that, on occasions which, happily, are few in number, the system breaks down.

The previous chapter finished with an historic reference to the failure of a man's proposed membership by virtue of the fact that five black balls were found in the ballot-box. This event was recorded by the then secretary in a seemingly humorous way but this kind of occurrence is uncharitable, unnecessary and not in keeping with the spirit of Freemasonry.

Only once, in all the years that I have been a Mason, have I been privy to such an event. This said, once was quite enough. I was not a member of the lodge in which it occurred. I was the proverbial "fly on the wall" by virtue of the fact that I was the "Guest Organist".

By coincidence, on the night in question, there were five black balls in the box. Though not directly involved, I found it debasing, distasteful and humiliating to all concerned.

When anyone is proposed for membership of my Mother Lodge, the members are circularised and asked whether, if such a proposal were made, any member would feel disposed to object. Any dissenter is then at liberty to contact the secretary in confidence, such dissent being the end of the matter.

This is, in effect, the ballot. The actual ballot taken in the Lodge is a pure formality and the harmony is never disturbed. In all the years of its existence, there has never been any instance of a black ball in The Lodge of St. Oswald in Shropshire.

Having mentioned my position as "Guest Organist" I would do an injustice to my fellow minstrels if I did not comment on our situation.

Organists and Guest Organists could well come under the heading of "Masonic Furniture." They are there to provide the music and are not always recognised as an integral part of the proceedings. If Guest Organists came any lower on the List of Officers, they would be getting orders for the printing.

One December, prior to the yuletide festivities, I was invited to Citizen Lodge in London, which Lodge was served by a very fine organist. I enjoyed both ceremony and the music which accompanied it. Subsequently, after a pint or two over which to contemplate the pleasures of a pleasant evening in convivial company, I joined my host, George for dinner.

The formalities of the evening took their course. In the fullness of time Grace and the National Anthem were sung, the music continuing to its previously high standard.

Towards the end of the meal my host left the table for a short time. On his return he requested that I go to the piano and , on his signal, play "Silent Night." There was an urgency in his voice that suggested he would wish me to accede to his request without delay. I therefore went to the piano and turned to watch George, who was now

I don't care if it is Xmas - No!

standing by the door. He was holding his hand aloft in the aspect of one who was about to start a race, a look of anticipation filling his face.

Presently his hand rose still further, then dropped. This was my signal to begin playing.

I did so. The lights went out! To rounds of applause from the members of the Lodge, four chefs entered the room bearing the traditional Christmas Pudding, ablaze in all its glory. The procession went twice round the room and retired through the door. As it did so, the lights were switched on again.

Having terminated my rendition of "Silent Night," I returned to my table to find my host awaiting me.

Having acknowledged his thanks I said, "George, you've got a very good organist in this lodge - why did you want me to play 'Silent Night'?"

"He plays everything from music. He can't play in the dark," said George.

I've enjoyed it! And, as I've already observed, the Provincial Grand Master of Sussex would wish us to enjoy our Masonry. He sets out to ensure that those under his direction not only fulfil the obligations which are expected of them, but enjoy themselves in the process. This end is achieved with no small degree of success.

There is an air of cordiality which pervades the Province of Sussex of which many other provinces might well feel envious. This is largely due to the fact that Sussex is a very popular retirement area, resulting in the intermingling of Masons from all over the country. They enjoy themselves, yet under the guidance of their Provincial Grand Master, they also observe the more formal occasions - not least the annual Church Service, when the Sussex Masons and their families come together in the presence of the Great Architect in non-Masonic surroundings.

So, what is Freemasonry? The question is asked on numerous occasions by those from the outside world. The answer is remarkably simple. Freemasonry is a form of entertainment. What form that entertainment takes is purely up to the individual, just as the interpretation of Freemasonry is a matter for the individual mind.

A game of football provides striker and goalkeeper with diametrically opposed views of success, failure and enjoyment. So Masonry provides its participants with a choice of how best to further their own enjoyment. (I must find out if that poor fellow is still secretary of three lodges!)

Different people react to situations in different ways. I once heard a man say he had "put his hands up and got a call from beyond" - A voice down the bar was heard to say "that the last man he knew who put his hands up got five years!"

We cannot expect our friends on the outside to have a full understanding of us simply because we do not fill in all the gaps before such time as they may join us. In many ways Masonry must seem an unlikely scenario.

"King Lear" was an unlikely scenario - a deranged old Monarch wandering round in circles with every conceivable family upset to boot - but, as with Masonry, Lear was entertaining. Not completely explicable - but entertaining nevertheless, in a grim sort of way.

Where therefore, we expect the non-Masonic world to be curious about us, we must allow their curiosity a degree of tolerance.

To this end, I am considering making application to join the Guildhall Lodge in London. And if, this having been achieved, in five or six years time I will have experienced Lord Mayoral regalia, a procession, transport by means of coach, various civic dignitaries in attendance, bands playing and luncheon at the Mansion House, then my whole thesis will have to be seen to be no longer valid. I will have to concede that a certain author was correct in his assumption that Masonry guarantees preferment.

In deference to my experiment however, one would hope that the said author would take his place in the crowd and wave his flag with everyone else. For my part it will be incumbent on me to admit a degree of error - but as they have already written one pantomime on this subject, I cannot see the exercise being repeated.

The writing of this book has left me with ambition. This is not as strange a reaction as may be first thought. I would like to visit a lodge in Bristol. I would like to cross Hadrian's Wall and enjoy the hospitality of our kilted Brethren in their own environment - somewhere in Glasgow is my father's old lodge. Without a doubt I would like to cross "The Pond," as airline jargon would have us refer to it, and see for myself the workings of Masonry in America. I do know those who have already enjoyed this experience. If the stories are to be believed, the warmth of the reception is quite breathtaking and the camaraderie encountered, second to none. It is consoling to know that Brother Benjamin Franklin did not get his way. He wanted to substitute the American Eagle for a turkey. The effect would not have been the same.

I would like to visit Australia. Down in Melbourne there is another Lodge of St. Oswald. It is the Sister Lodge of my Mother Lodge and is a venue I have always wanted to visit. At every meeting of St. Oswald's Lodge in Shropshire the members sing a song to their visitors. The words were provided by their Brothers "down under," the song being sung to the tune of "Waltzing Matilda." This is a piece of nostalgia it has always been my pleasure to recall when the number of miles between home and me has seemed somewhat great.

Although no longer possible, I would have liked to visit P.2. Lodge in Italy. Pure curiosity, though I do not doubt that the welcome would have been most cordial. Although not in his jurisdiction, our own Grand Master may have had similar ideas. He may well have pondered the prospect of a Continental trip encompassing a visit to the Brethren of P.2. For their part, they would have, no doubt, been very taken with the idea of "The Dook" coming for dinner.

Throughout this book I have, on more than the odd occasion, referred to our Masonic Topers. It would be remiss of me not to invite them to participate in the finale. Throughout my observations, I have continually made the point that all situations have more than one vantage point. To this end I recount the episode of the West Country Provincial Grand Master who visited a Temperance Lodge within his Province.

Although Temperance Lodges were originally founded with the said object in mind, maturity has allowed latitude of attitude and abstinence has become a matter of individual conscience.

On the occasion recalled, once the formalities had been concluded in the lodge, the Provincial Grand Master made his way to the Festive Board. Upon enquiry he indicated that he would like a drink of alcoholic content. He was re-appraised with the fact he was visiting a Temperance Lodge and told that alcoholic drinks were not served.

Slightly bemused, the Head of the Province made the point that the provision of alcoholic drinks for *guests* surely featured in the catering arrangements.

Sadly, for the distinguished visitor, this was not the case. The Provincial Grand Master had to drink orange-juice. He said he would not return to that lodge - and never did!

Sometimes the quenching of thirst in the desert is as impossible as a camp-fire in the Monsoon Season.

Whereas we must allow the interpretation of Masonry to be the prerogative of the individual, on more than one occasion I have been witness to people reading too much into it. Here I am referring to both Masons and non-Masons. Conversely, it is a dangerous course to take anything, not just Masonry, at face value. Consider another reported instance in 1992.

"Clive R...... of Maidstone was banned for 21 days and fined £150 for doing 104 m.p.h. on the M.20. Chris A...... was stopped for exceeding 70 m.p.h. in the Scottish Highlands and received a caution."

Nothing too startling one would think - until one learns that Master Clive was driving a three-wheeled Reliant Robin and Friend Chris was riding a push-bike!

In the same year British Rail announced that "any train running less than an hour late would be deemed to be running on time" - and the Belfast Telegraph reported that "83% of cars coming into the City centre had only one driver."

In retrospect, those who got the wrong impression of Masonry can be forgiven. To get the wrong ideas on any subject is easy, by not fully understanding all the facts. Even a simple, pragmatic statement can be misconstrued. The proprietor of our local Chinese Take-Away announced that "we would not see him for a fortnight as he was going home."

It was enquired of him if China were not a long way to be going for a fortnight. He replied, "Not gonna China - gonna Coventry!"

Even within the membership, ideas on Masonry differ. In the chapter on our Colonial Cousins I made reference to the demonstrative wearing of Masonic emblems. My own Masonic upbringing was in the school of thought which deters such practice. This said, it is not for me to question the thinking of my fellows. One Brother in my locality turned up at meetings looking like a Masonic Christmas Tree - Masonic emblems everywhere! Grant him the choice. I have always said that he must have provided the archetype for the prime character in the TV series, "Minder."

There are those Masons who get the system wrong - but then in this world, it is not only the Masons who get things wrong. In Port Huron, Michigan, they expelled poor old Thomas Edison from school because they thought he was retarded. This act of injustice was the result of his being partially deaf due to a bout of Scarlet Fever.

There are those Masons who join, and after a time, stop attending. Unless there is some underlying factor involved, the reason for this is quite simple. They have stopped enjoying themselves. This is not necessarily the fault of Freemasonry. They have just run out of steam.

**Whether or not you enjoyed your evening
deputizing with the Mission Hall Jazz Band
has got nothing to do with it. - We don't want
to hear "One more time" at the end of the
Opening Ode again!**

There are those Masons who expect too much - few and far between - but they do exist. They are usually given short shrift. I was privy to a conversation between an old hand and a newly joined Brother, when the newly joined Brother made a preposterous request he felt should be gratified simply because he had joined our ranks. He was referred, by his venerable companion, to the services of a taxidermist! - But, I would hasten to add, in defence of the aforementioned venerable companion, that the taxidermist came highly recommended and was of the highest professional standing.

There are those Masons to whom I will raise my glass tonight. The curtain is about to come down on my performance, thus, as an erstwhile theatrical, it is with gratitude that I will thank my audience in the accepted form. The Masons to whom I will first raise my glass tonight are my fellow topers - but having acknowledged them, and my place among their ranks, let me not forget my fellow Masons everywhere. Most importantly, having done that, may my final toast be to all those of you in the world who have made this journey with me. May the Great Architect allow you health, happiness and everything else that you may wish yourselves.

No, good reader, we're not a funny bunch of people - but some of us do have a sense of humour!